Doing Work You Love

Doing

Work

You

Love

Discovering Your Purpose and Realizing Your Dreams

CHERYL GILMAN

CB

CONTEMPORARY BOOKS

Library of Congress Cataloging-in-Publication Data

Gilman, Cheryl.
    Doing work you love : discovering your purpose and realizing your dreams /
Cheryl Gilman.
        p.   cm.
    ISBN 0-8092-3043-7
      1. Career development.   2. Vocational interests.   3. Creative ability.
    4. Achievement motivation.   5. Self-realization.   I. Title.
    HF5381.G534   1997
    650.1—dc21   97-15763
                                              CIP

Excerpt from W. Bridges, *Transitions: Making Sense of Life's Changes*, copyright
© 1980 by Addison-Wesley Publishing Company Inc., reprinted by permission of
Addison-Wesley Longman Inc.

Excerpt from Jack Canfield and Mark Victor Hansen, *Chicken Soup for the Soul*,
copyright © 1993 by Health Communications, reprinted by permission of the
publisher.

Excerpt from Paul and Sarah Edwards, *Finding Your Perfect Work*, copyright
© 1996 by Paul and Sarah Edwards, reprinted by permission of Putnam
Publishing Company.

Excerpt from Faith Popcorn, *Clicking*, copyright © 1996 by Faith Popcorn and Lys
Marigold, reprinted by permission of HarperCollins Publishers, Inc.

Excerpts from Michael Ray and Rochelle Myers, *Creativity in Business*, and from
Joseph Campbell and Bill Moyers, *The Power of Myth*, reprinted by permission of
Bantam Doubleday Dell Publishing Group, Inc.

Cover design by Scott Rattray
Cover illustration copyright © Frédéric Joos/Stock Illustration Source
Interior design by Jeanette Wojtyla

Published by Contemporary Books
A division of NTC/Contemporary Publishing Group, Inc.
4255 West Touhy Avenue, Lincolnwood (Chicago), Illinois 60712-1975 U.S.A.
Copyright © 1997 by Cheryl Gilman
Printed in the United States of America
International Standard Book Number: 0-8092-3043-7
01 02 03 04 05 06 QB 22 21 20 19 18 17 16 15 14 13 12 11 10 9 8 7 6 5 4

To Sara and Adam

Contents

Acknowledgments

There are many people I gratefully acknowledge for making this book a possibility: first, my writing coach, Kathleen Redmond, and my agent, Jim Levine, without whose encouragement I would not have begun. I especially thank Kara Leverte and Contemporary Books for believing in and publishing *Doing Work You Love*. Special thanks to my terrific editors, Susan Schwartz and Alissa Macmillan, both for their enthusiasm as well as their many perceptive suggestions.

I particularly want to thank Interface in Cambridge and Newton, Massachusetts, for supporting my vision and sponsoring my seminars.

I give many thanks to Lynn Robinson and Margaret Newhouse, who also patiently read and courageously red-penciled the work in process. I want to acknowledge Colquit Meachem for her inspiration and support during the early stages of writing this book.

Most of all I want to thank my children, Sara and Adam, whom I was privileged to parent, and all the wonderful people I've had the opportunity to work with over the years: my students, clients, coworkers, and managers. You have all been my real teachers. It's because of your courage, insights, and experiences that this book has come to be.

Dear Reader

We are in the midst of a major revolution in the way we work and live. The United States and other industrialized countries are undergoing cultural upheavals. Family and work structures, the icons and certainties we grew up with, no longer exist. The transition to the Information Age has brought with it new opportunities as well as confusion about the future and fear of the unknown. Over 50 percent of the products and services that will be introduced in the next decade haven't been invented yet. As we approach the millennium we are undergoing a tidal wave of uncertainty. We are redefining the way we work and relate, our roles and rules. In 1776 we were promised "life, liberty, and the pursuit of happiness." This was a new promise for humankind. We still believe it, want it, and expect it. Prior to the Great Depression, there were no entitlements, retirement, benefits, or weekends. We are now returning to an era of no entitlements, retirement, benefits, or weekends. And we don't like it! We are in the process of re-creating our way of living and working.

We live in a culture of mixed messages. Our spiritual values say we are more than what we do while at the same time we define ourselves by our work, our titles, how much money we make, what kind of car we drive. We are endlessly goal-driven. We are told we have unlimited opportunities and that we can be anything we want to be. This is not only a myth but also a paralyzing burden. Since 1979 there have been more than 43 million layoffs in the United States and they are continuing. Job stress is one of the top work-related health problems in America. Since what we choose today may disappear tomorrow, as so many have realized, what is the answer? There is only one: Do work you love that allows you to keep expanding your natural talents and passions and adapt *those* to the marketplace. This is your only security in a world without certainties. It supports who you are in a culture where you are defined by what you do, where job stress is a killer, and where relationships and values fall apart when you bring work stress to them.

I wrote this book because I wanted to give you the information I use in my Doing Work You Love seminars. When I first proposed my seminar to an organization in 1993, they declined. They said they could never fill career workshops. I persisted because I knew there was a need. They finally said yes. It *sold out* on the first night. People from all professions came to that seminar and those that followed. They were in health care, architecture, law, education, business, and engineering. They said they were unhappy, bored, or burned out. They were angry that they had been lied to, that they were working harder than ever and feeling more and more insecure. Mothers called me to coach their college-age children. They wanted to help their kids make the right decision. There were others who were reentering the job market. They wanted more satisfying work as well as earning a living; they wanted to have more control and balance in their lives. They wanted a rest. They didn't know what to do next and had given up dreaming. Almost.

They left the Doing Work You Love seminars with "ahas" and a new way of looking at things. One person said it was as if a veil of superstition had been lifted. I asked them what was different about this approach. They said it was the clarity, the lack of BS. They said the seminar was rooted in the here and now, that I understood their responsibilities and their concerns because I had been there. They saw they had talents that they hadn't thought of as marketable. They learned where to go for help and resources and the nitty-gritty steps on *how* to "just do it." They shared fears, war stories, and successes. They saw they weren't alone. You will read some of their stories as well as what they and others did to improve their careers and lives.

Doing Work You Love has been written to help you start living your future now. You will:

- *Uncover myths about work that you believe but aren't true.* Myths such as "You have to be good at one thing for your whole life" are so ingrained in our thinking that we don't recognize them or the power they hold over us. This book will help you let go of beliefs that are keeping you back.
- *Uncover the skills you have but were taught to deny.* Many of us were raised to focus on what we *don't* do well. If we were good in English but not in math, we were told to focus on math. If we were good in art but not in science, we were told to pay more attention to science. We were taught to diminish our strengths and mold ourselves into the safest career. You will learn to expand your natural talents and passions in your work *and* earn a living.
- *Uncover your passions and your purpose.* We long to make a difference, to contribute to others, and to feel that our lives have meaning. This often feels like one more complex mystery to unravel. You will learn how to simplify the process and discover your life's purpose.

This book is designed to help you find work you love doing in today's world. You can use it as if you were taking my seminar. You can do this alone, with a friend, or with a team. My intention for you is that you will:

- *Find or create a new job that fits you and your passion.* You are unique. There is no one else like you, with your talents and skills, with your interests and experience. You will learn how to overcome the fears that keep you from moving ahead, as well as ways to spark your creative thinking to expand your work possibilities.
- *Do work you love in the job you now have.* You may not have to change jobs. You will learn to think of yourself differently— with more control and more choices. You will read about people in my seminars who discovered they really *liked* what they were doing; you'll read about others who created new jobs within their companies.

- *Help your kids choose work they will love too.* In a world where even traditional occupations such as law, medicine, and teaching are no longer secure, parents are often baffled about how to advise their children. *Doing Work You Love* will support you in helping your kids embark on their life's work.

We are all in this together. One of the joys of the work I do is the wonderful people I meet who share their stories. I welcome *your* stories. Please send them to me. The more we celebrate who we are and expand our gifts, the more we can support each other. As we approach the new millennium, let's envision a world where we all work hard at what we love doing. That's where we make our real contribution. That's the real definition of success!

Preface

Since 1979 there have been more than 43 million layoffs in the United States, and they are continuing.

Although one-half of companies reported an increase in profits, 86 percent saw a decline in employee morale.

Job stress is one of the top work-related health problems in America.

Most heart attacks happen Monday morning before 9:00 A.M.

In 1776 we were promised "life, liberty, and the pursuit of happiness." This was a new promise for humankind.

We live in a work-centered, career-oriented, financially driven culture.

We yearn for richer, simpler lives with more meaning and soul.

Introduction

"Real success is working hard at what you love."
Michael Ray and Rochelle Myers,
Creativity in Business

I've been lucky. I say this with gratitude. I've had second, third, and sixth chances. On my *frequently* changing career paths, I've been able to talk to thousands of people around the world. I've been a teacher, a secretary, and a headhunter. I've been a researcher, a salesperson, and an entrepreneur. I've had jobs that lasted two weeks and jobs that lasted years. I've been broke and I've had money. I've left companies that didn't support my goals, and I've been laid off from those that filed for Chapter II. I often vacillated between total despair and action. I was a senior manager for a large corporation, and I raised two wonderful children alone. My protected, middle-class "princess" education had not prepared me for any of it. I learned by being ignorant about what I wasn't supposed to do, by not understanding what the word *no* meant, and by being desperate to provide for my family.

At 28 with a two- and a three-year-old, I was on my own. I had no plan, no experience save a few earlier years of teaching, absolutely no understanding of how the world worked, and very limited self-esteem. I used the misinformation and beliefs available to me to define myself and to get jobs. I worked all the time. I regret most not having been able to spend more time with my children. They will tell you I was always there. Perception is everything. It was my loss.

Over the years, I saw people stuck in jobs they hated, believing they had no choice, and I also saw others who loved what they did. I witnessed (and experienced) abusive managers and a few supportive ones. I saw educated adults put up with outrageous behavior. I listened to them tell me they had no choice, "this is the way the world works." I also met people who were doing what they loved and had carved out passionate careers that brought joy to themselves and to others. I learned how to change careers that no longer supported me, how to get the interview, and how to be successful in jobs for which I wasn't trained.

I was fortunate to have worked for one company that was committed to growing people as well as business. They provided me with responsibilities, status, travel, and a salary I never would have dreamed of. Then the marketplace changed. Seemingly overnight, this company changed too. Workaholism, technology, and the bottom line were the only values that remained. That company was not unique. As the company downsized tens of thousands of employees, I saw colleagues become traumatized and ill as they waited for the ax to fall. They had given their lives to that company. Their world had fallen apart. They hadn't looked for a job in 25 years and they doubted their own value.

I didn't want another job when I left. The thought of looking for another j•o•b filled me with dread—not because I didn't know how; I knew that only too well. But because I might *find* one and then possibly be laid off once more. Only this time I'd be even older.

My body had been screaming at me for years to stop. Along with the increased opportunities at this company, I had also developed continuous muscle spasms and pinched nerves. Although I heard what my body was trying to tell me, I felt powerless. I had become a driven workaholic, and didn't know where I was going. I had forgotten who I was and suddenly I didn't know what I'd do next. How would I support myself if I wasn't doing that job? My father had died of a heart attack from job stress. I only knew that this time I needed to pay attention and change in order to survive.

I slowed down long enough to heal. I started simplifying my life and paying attention to what was really important to me; what sparked me; how I wanted to live; and how I could use my gifts, skills, experience, and interests in the next part of my life. I was creating a vision for my future. I decided to put my energy toward educating people and empowering them in their work—an area where I had struggled so much. I would teach them what I had learned—how to have the best work for themselves wherever they are; how to ask for what they want; how to have options; how to interview; how to manage stress and stay motivated; how to coach their kids, their friends, and themselves. I would also teach that we had gotten it wrong and it wasn't our fault. Much of it was cultural. There was still time. I read books about people who had started new careers at 40, 50, and 60. I talked to men and women who had left corporations and had created successful businesses that allowed them flexible schedules. I spoke with people who were telecommuting so that they could be with their children. I coached clients on the importance of valuing themselves, recognizing what they already had, and helped them develop the tools they needed to do the work they loved. I created Doing Work You Love seminars, which continually evolve because of the thousands of wonderful people who come to them.

And, yes, I have created work that I love. It's work that has given me a new beginning, a sense of joy and meaning, where I am surrounded by positive, supportive, loving people and where I can give back. I want the same for you.

Doing Work You Love will give you information and instructions you can try on to see how they fit—just as if you were trying on new clothes. They've worked for me and many others. Use what feels comfortable. Adjust them to your style and needs.

This is a small book. I've tried to keep it simple. Keep notes. An inexpensive spiral notebook works best—one you don't mind messing up. At the back of this book there is a reference list of other books and tapes to support you on your path. Be patient with yourself; change takes time.

Keep the aphorisms with you as daily reminders. I hope you gain not only new understandings but practical techniques you can use. I'd love to hear from you. Please drop me a line at this address:

Cheryl Gilman Associates
46 Choate Road
Belmont, MA 02178

Enjoy. Remember, this isn't a dress rehearsal. It's all we've got. And besides, since we're going to have to work hard anyway, we may as well work hard at what we love!

Start Where You Are

∞∞∞

"We already have everything we need.
There is no need for self-improvement."

Pema Chodron,
Start Where You Are

Everything you have done until now
has been your training—for the rest of
your life.

The Truth About You

"One of the most important results you can bring into the world is the you that you really want to be."
Robert Fritz

A *gift* is something you are born with. It's something you can
do that's as easy as breathing.
A *skill* is something you learn to do. It may draw upon your
gifts.
An *interest* is something that draws you, that speaks to you.
An *experience* is an emotional or mental perception that you
have or something physical that you have done.

Contrary to popular belief, you do not need to change, be fixed,
or improve. You are unique and perfect just the way you are.
You know everything you need to know. You just forgot. Tests
won't tell you who you are or what you should be. They'll just
confirm what you already know.

We live in a curious culture. We are taught to focus on what
we're not good at. Perhaps our Puritan background is still influ-
encing us more than we'd like to admit.

When we were children in school, we were told that if we
were good at English but not at math, we needed to concentrate
on math (or vice versa). Or if we were good at art but not in science, we needed to work harder on science. Since what we focus
on expands, we were continually paying attention to our weak-
nesses rather than our strengths. Many of us learned when we
were young *not* to value what was easy. Couple that with the
need to conform and fit in (strong motivators in school), the
need to be liked, and the need to protect ourselves from the
thousand subtle attacks that are part of growing up in our culture. It is little wonder that many of us came to believe there is
something *wrong* with us. We are taught that if it's too easy it's
not important. Advertising understands this perfectly! It continues to lure us to buy this or that product to improve who we

are. Advertisers know we think there's something missing. If we would only buy their product or service, we would become thinner, richer, sexier, smarter, and happier. We'd have more fun and everyone would love us!

What if we were to focus instead on what is easy, effortless, and enjoyable and become really good at that? And let others do the same. That doesn't mean we wouldn't work hard. We would work hard at what we love doing. Einstein didn't write operas and Mozart wasn't a scientist. And we didn't know we needed them until they did what they did.

Michael Ray, professor of the popular Creativity in Business program at Stanford University and coauthor with Rochelle Myers of the book with the same title, says that "the goal of living with EEE (easy, effortless, and enjoyable) is ease, effortlessness, and enjoyment. Surprisingly, EEE turns into a discipline for achieving a higher goal: the discovery of your true purpose in life. Each individual has a meant-to-be, a particular blending of talents and capacities that can guide him to achievement."[1]

To create work you love, pay attention to what feeds you and to what nourishes your soul. Focus on what *you* have felt most satisfied doing regardless of what others have said you *should* feel. Let others who are good at the rest *do* the rest. Expand and amplify your gifts. Hone other skills that you must have and give what's left away.

Try This:

To see where you are doing work that you love now, answer these questions:

1. What is easy and effortless for you to do? What's as easy as breathing? Where and when are you doing it now? These are your gifts.

2. What was the first thing you ever did that you thought was fun, that you really enjoyed, that you felt special at, or that really "turned you on"? (Whatever image or thought that comes to you first is the answer.) What did you like about it? How are you doing that now? These are your gifts.

3. What was the first job you ever had (either paid or unpaid) that you really enjoyed? What did you love about it and what gives you that same kind of feeling now? These are your gifts. Honor them.

4. Look at what you hate doing, procrastinate on, or are constantly struggling with. Write these things down. Choose one thing from that list and *delegate it to someone else.*

Example:

I hate to read instruction manuals. I've given up kidding myself that someday I'll learn to like them. I'd rather spend my time writing, coaching, and designing seminars—things that I enjoy and am good at. When I decided to produce a newsletter, I hired Mary Wilson to do the desktop publishing. I knew I had the *ability* to understand and use the manuals that come with newsletter software. However, the time it would have taken me to do that—along with my resistance—would have delayed the results (indefinitely in my mind). Mary is a musician and piano teacher who also has a small desktop-publishing business. She had the patience and attention to detail (that I didn't) to format the material I gave her. She also input thousands of names and addresses into a database I could use later. Not only was she good at what she did, but she was also a joy to work with.

Where in your life can you ask someone else to do what you resist doing—a change that will support *both* of you?

"Do you want to be really happy? You can start by being appreciative of who you are and what you've got."
The Tao of Pooh, Benjamin Hoff

What They Said About Working Then Are Myths Today

A myth is something that was once firmly believed but is no longer true. It is so strongly ingrained into our way of thinking that we don't recognize it for what it is. We were born into our myths unknowingly.

One of the myths I grew up with was that men were the breadwinners and women took care of the home. I learned that besides being wives and mothers, women could sometimes be teachers, social workers, nurses, secretaries, or flight attendants—but only if they weren't married or if their husbands died. While I believed this to be the way of the world, I also dreamed of being a ballerina, a teacher, a nurse, a pilot, an actress, a singer, Annie Oakley, a model, a writer, an artist, a doctor, a telephone repairperson, a trapeze artist, and more!

Today over 60 percent of American women with school-age children work outside the home in jobs as varied as telephone repairperson to U.S. senator. There are as many people working for businesses owned by women as there are working for Fortune 500 companies.

Here are some more myths you may or may not be carrying around with you:

- *Myth: If you go to school, you are assured a good job you can grow with.* That was true 20 years ago. Today, you can expect to have 6 to 10 different jobs in your career, and it is unlikely that any two of them will be with the same company.
- *Myth: Go to work for a big company. If you work hard and are loyal, they'll take care of you.* That's true as long as they need you. Now you are the one responsible for your welfare. Among the 24 million enterprises in the United States only 7,000 have more than 500 employees. The majority of the others have fewer than five.

- *You can be anything you want to be.* You can't. You can only be "what is in harmony with what you were designed to be," write Arthur Miller and Ralph Mattson in their classic *The Truth About You.* They interviewed more than 3,000 people and found "there was not one exception. Pressures from family, education, the culture and media notwithstanding, the data held true. That which motivated you when you were young continues to motivate you."[2] Stress and disease come when you are in conflict with that design. Your vitality and your contribution come from those gifts and motivations that are authentically yours.
- *Myth: You have unlimited potential.* You don't. You have potential. And you have limitations. If you weren't born rich, safe, supported, loved, in great health and shape, white, male, tall, handsome (with hair!), smart, outgoing, and from a social, nondysfunctional family, you have different limitations, self-perceptions, and challenges than someone who was. The question is "How are *you* going to use *your* talents and have your dreams with *your* potential within *your* limitations?"

Here are just a few more messages you may have heard about work:

Women with kids don't work.
Settle down into one job.
Never quit until you have another job.
The best time to look for a job is when you have a job.
Be grateful that you have any job.
Work = Worth.
Compete and win at all costs.
Work is a duty—not for self-fulfillment.
Your work is your identity.
Lots of change means there's something wrong.
Make sure you make yourself fit into what they want.
Your employer will take care of you.
You have to be able to do one thing well and do it for your life.
If it's too easy or fun it's not work—shame on you!

You need to struggle.
The boss is always right.
You can only be a _____.
It is important that you are a _____.

Try This:

On a clean sheet of paper, make a list of some of the myths you used to believe and some that you still hold. Remember—a myth is something that was once firmly believed but is no longer true, no matter how much you would like it to be.

Rate each of these myths from 1 to 10 according to how strongly you believed it was true when it may have had some validity and how strongly you believe it now. (1 = didn't/don't strongly believe, 5 = sometimes believe(d), 10 = base(d) my life on it.) For example:

Myth	Before	Now
Men work. Women stay at home.	10	2
I have unlimited potential.	7	1

The Truth About Work

"Work = activity. Some work is for fee. Some isn't."
Charles Handy

What is the difference between working and playing? Some say you are paid for working, you aren't paid for playing. Others say that playing is fun and working isn't.

Is a professional basketball star working or playing when he's on the court? How about city kids "playing" ball after school with the intention of becoming basketball stars? Are they playing or working? What about a homemaker who doesn't receive a salary for the thousands of tasks she performs each day? Is she working or playing? She isn't being paid for her job, and would she call it fun?

What differentiates work from play is *you* saying so.

Try Answering These:

1. When is work fun? When do you enjoy your work? What do you like about it? (Include such things as location, people, your manager, hours, flexibility, structure, nonstructure, benefits, culture, paycheck, etc.)
2. What do you hate about your job? (You can use the previous list here too.)

The need to have work we love grows as we become older. Not having it can result in paralysis of the spirit.

You Are Always Right

Do you want to be right, or do you want to be happy?

We will do almost anything to prove ourselves right. We will find justification, reasons, "truths," and examples of how what we believe is so. We will go to war to prove ourselves right.

If you say there is no way you could have work that you love, you will be right. If you say there is a way, you will also be right. If you continue to complain about a job that makes you unhappy year after year because you cannot do the type of work you want to in that company, then you are right. You can't and won't be happy there.

When my son, Adam, was graduating from college, Massachusetts was in the midst of a high-tech depression. The job market looked pretty bleak. Companies were laying off tens of thousands of people. "Everyone" said that there were no jobs out there—especially for a new graduate. Adam wasn't very excited by any of the jobs he was interviewing for when the corporate recruiters came to campus. He also wasn't getting second interviews. Adam had high grades and good work experience, and was very personable. He felt dejected. It is always puzzling to me when we are disappointed by not getting what we don't want in the first place! Of course, he, like many of us, had been told to go after the job, *any* job, and get the offer. After all, the advice went, you can always say no later. Just get the offer. It doesn't matter if you want the job or not. Particularly if you believe there are few available jobs.

How many people have been stuck in jobs for years because they fell into work they didn't really want? It's better to focus on what you want and not waste your time on years of pain and dissatisfaction. I coached Adam to wait until September to begin his job search. By that time the hordes of job-seeking seniors would have thinned out. He would have the summer to play or to work at something other than his career. He could begin anew in the fall. He believed there were lots of opportunities out there for him—they just weren't coming to Amherst.

When September came, Adam had a plan. He had also had a great summer. While in college, he had majored in marketing. His goal was to be a marketing consultant. He knew that to do this he needed experience in sales. Besides, he wanted to make money! He decided he would look for a successful company that would provide him with the training he needed. He also knew he wanted to work with upbeat, proactive people in a professional environment that was located in eastern Massachusetts. Six weeks after beginning his campaign, Adam was working as the youngest sales exec for the New England regional branch of a Fortune 500 company. He got the training and support he needed and, two years later, he was one of their top sales reps.

Try These:

1. When are you more committed to being right rather than being happy? Think about what you complain about the most. How could you change that?
2. Whenever you find yourself with a negative belief that will keep you from having what you want, say "switch" and restate it in the positive.

Example: "There are no jobs."

Switch: "There *is* a perfect job for what I want to do and I'm going to find it." (All you need is one!)

Your Life Is Your Career

"**Career** 1. a chosen pursuit; a profession or occupation. 2. the general course or progression of one's life."

"**Careerism** the practice of seeking one's professional advancement by all possible means."

American Heritage Dictionary,
Second College Edition

We have deified careers to such an extent that they end up driving us, rather than we them. We have become worshippers at the altar of careerism.

You are unique. There is no one else on this planet who is exactly like you. There isn't anyone anywhere with your composite of gifts, talents, skills, interests, and life experiences. There is no one who has learned to survive and succeed the way you have. If you made it through high school, you have succeeded. School is the great leveler, the great conformer. It was not only within your family that you learned survival skills, but also on the playground and in the school corridors. This was your training for the "real world." The skills you developed are now part of your strengths, your power. We'll talk more about them later.

I was shy as a child. I didn't know what to say to people. My father wanted me to be sociable. He told me that "an interested person is an interesting person." I wasn't sure what that meant, but somehow it was the key that pushed me to ask questions. I learned at an early age that if I asked people about themselves, they would like me. Everyone likes to talk about themselves. I have been interviewing people since I can remember. Sometimes I'm even paid to do this.

Your life is your career. Everything that you have experienced is part of *your* resource list. Your wealth is in your gifts, talents, skills, experiences, and interests as well as your struggles. Your job is to choose which one of these you want to use next.

Try These:

1. List as many of your gifts as you can (at least 10) and rate them by how much you enjoy using them. Circle the top three. (Remember, gifts are things you can do that come as easily as breathing.)

   Example:

   Some of my gifts are listening, teaching, reading, writing, painting, being intuitive, eating, sleeping, breathing, being still, dancing, speaking to large groups of people, learning a foreign language. Organizing—making order out of chaos—is *not* one of my talents. When I redid my office, I was paralyzed by the mess. My daughter, Sara, knew this about me. She sent me out of the house so she could rearrange everything. She then sat with me to help me create the systems that I needed. Maybe organizing is one of your gifts too. If so, I need you.

2. List as many skills as you can and rate them by how much you enjoy them. Underline the top four or five. (Remember, a skill is something you learned to do. Skills can be enhanced gifts too.)

Example:

Some of my skills are typing, editing, writing, coaching, cooking, analyzing, teaching, interviewing. I've underlined my top four from this list. Although I enjoy cooking, I'm not passionate about it and wouldn't want to earn my living doing it.

3. List your interests. Include current interests as well as those you had when you were younger. Underline those that you want to include in your life now. Then circle the top four or five. Don't worry if you can't think of too many. We'll do more uncovering later.

4. On a clean sheet of paper, make a list of your top skills and interests. For example, some of mine are:

Skills	Interests
Writing	Personal development
Coaching	Europe
Teaching	Art
Interviewing	International cultures

What are yours?

You Don't Know What You Don't Know (How Could You?)

We often act as if we know everything there is to know. Oh, we'll deny this. We'll say, "Of course I don't know everything."

However, our actions say something different. We design our lives on the basis of beliefs, opinions, and fears about what might happen if we don't do what we are currently doing. But there is no way we can know what will happen! *We have very limited knowledge.*

The light bulb represents all the knowledge in the world. The tip of the light bulb (A) depicts everything *you know.* The base (B) is everything *you know you don't know.* (You know you don't know how to sail a boat or you know you don't understand quantum physics, etc.) The rest (C) reflects what *you don't know you don't know.* It is outside the realm of your comprehension of your possibilities.

Try This:

1. On a clean piece of paper, make a list of all the things you've dreamed of doing or being. Fantasize. Don't judge them as being foolish or silly. Just write them down.

2. Choose one thing from your list and state all the reasons you couldn't be, do, or have it. How do you know you couldn't? Elaborate. Who said so? How did *they* know?
3. Next state all the reasons you might be able to have exactly what you want.
4. Choose another item from your list. Repeat steps 2 and 3.
5. Now look at your list and try to pick out the themes. Cluster your dreams around the feelings you might have if those dreams were to come true or the qualities they represent for you.

Example:

I wanted to be a ballerina, a choreographer, an actress, an artist, a writer, a teacher, a nurse, a translator in the United Nations, a wife, a mother, an international traveler, a public speaker, a French professor, a bookstore owner, a boutique owner, a model, a gallery owner, and a clothing designer. My common themes are: visibility, creativity, nurturing, autonomy, art, books, international involvement, *and* variety.

Visibility: ballerina, actress, public speaker, teacher, professor, writer, model
Creativity: choreographer, writer, actress, artist, teacher, public speaker, clothing designer
Nurturing: teacher, nurse, wife, mother
International involvement: French professor, international traveler, translator in the United Nations
Autonomy: gallery owner, clothing designer, a boutique/bookstore owner

What about you? What themes were prevelant on your list? Did you dream of working with your hands with tools, plants, the earth, materials, or fabrics? Did you see yourself happily working by yourself or with groups of people? Did you desire to be physically active or a star or a leader? Did you imagine yourself as a scientist or an inventor, a researcher or a philosopher? Was being rich a common theme? What about doing good works, changing the world, or living in nature? On a clean sheet of paper, list your top three to five qualities. For example, here's my list:

Qualities
1. Visibility
2. Creativity
3. Nurturing
4. Autonomy
5. Variety

How Much Do You *Really* Earn?

"It was such a tough day that I deserve a little fun. Let's go out to dinner/dancing/a movie/the mall."

Your Money or Your Life, Joe
Dominguez and Vicki Robin[3]

It wasn't until I read *Your Money or Your Life* by Joe Dominguez and Vicki Robin that I realized how much I had been *paying* to work. Their wonderful (and sobering) book helped me see where my large salary was disappearing. Yes, my job had been *costing* me money! Although I was earning more than I had ever dreamed possible, I could never understand why I had so little left at the end of the month. I was also working *all* the time. I usually didn't leave the office before 7:00 P.M. and always brought work home at night and on weekends. If I was doing business with Asia or Europe, I would often make phone calls after midnight. If I wasn't at my job, I was commuting to it, traveling for it, or planning, thinking, and worrying about it. And I wasn't unique—my colleagues were doing the same. That 40 to 50 hour a week job quickly became 60 to 70 hours of personal energy each week!

I knew my life was out of balance but I also thought I could handle it. When the yoga and meditation I had practiced since my early twenties didn't cure the pinched nerves and muscle spasms, I went to physicians, chiropractors, acupuncturists, and to massage therapists, physical therapists, and psychotherapists. Sometimes they helped; sometimes scotch was faster. I felt I was holding myself together with tape and paper clips. I also believed that if I looked good, I would feel better too. So when I wasn't working or seeing doctors, I was shopping. "Oh, just this one thing. It's such a good buy, and besides, the kids or I need it." Or occasionally we would eat at some wonderful new restaurant. "Not often," I reasoned. "And besides, I deserve it. Don't I work all the time?!"

Dominguez and Robin say that "Money is something we choose to trade our life energy for." Although I was earning close to six figures, when I did the following exercise[4], I saw that I was trading my life energy for around $5.25 per hour. That was what I was *really* earning although I paid taxes on much, much more. It was no wonder I had so little left at the end of the month.

How about you? How much are *you* paying for your job?

Try These:

To find your *real* hourly wage, answer these questions:

1. *What is your current hourly wage based on your present weekly income?* If you earn $1,000 per week for a 40-hour-a-week job, your hourly wage is $25. If you are really spending 50 hours at the office and another 10 hours in work-related activities (e.g., conferences, dinners out, networking, thinking, or worrying), add this to your workweek. Your hourly wage is now $16.67.

2. *How much time and money do you spend commuting?* If you spend an hour and a half commuting each day, add 7.5 hours to

your total workweek. Now you are earning $14.80. You will also want to subtract transportation costs (automobile, insurance, taxis, buses, metro trains, etc.).

3. *How much are you spending on meals (e.g., lunches and dinners out—either alone or with colleagues)?*

4. *How much time and income are you spending to relieve the stress you are enduring?* Is the television your escape mode of choice or do you prefer to shop? Add the number of hours you spend in front of the tube or in any other activity that helps you manage an unsatisfying and stressful job. Let's say it's a conservative five hours. Your hourly wage is now $13.80, and we haven't even factored in what you've bought during all those visits to the mall.

5. *How much do you spend on clothing?* Do you like the clothes you buy for work? Are they the same that you would choose if you weren't doing this job? If not, subtract that too.

6. *How many of your illnesses are work- or stress-related?* Do you seek professional help that is beyond what your managed health care plan provides? Or do you drink to manage the pain? How much do these extras cost you weekly? How much time do you spend in doctors' offices or at home recovering? Include all of these in your calculations too.

    One of my friends, a highly respected manager, was frequently out sick. The higher the stress levels, the more often he was absent. He had severe colds, bronchitis, stomach and back problems, flus, migraines, and even food poisoning. He didn't need to fabricate the symptoms, sometimes he could barely talk or move. On the weekends, when he was better, he drank vodka.

7. *What about association dues, meetings, and conferences?* Or courses and programs that you need to go to rather than those that really interest you? Include time spent as well as membership and dinner fees not paid for by your company.

8. *Add all the job-related hours to your normal workweek and subtract the job-related expenses from your usual pay.* What is your *real*

hourly wage today? And what percentage of *that* do you pay in taxes?

Now think about this: What if every day you did work you loved and that you were proud of? What if it gave you a sense of deep satisfaction and joy where you knew you were making a real contribution? What would you need to spend your money on then?

Get Rid of the Baggage

"First there is an ending, then a beginning, with an important empty or fallow time in between. That is the order of things in nature. Leaf fall, winter, and then the green emerges again from the dry brown wood. Human affairs would flow along similar channels if we were better able to stay in the current."
William Bridges, *Transitions*

"You have to have emptiness before it can be filled. You have to exhale before you can inhale."
Tom Yeomans

In this time of never-ending goal setting, overwork, and infor-mation glut, simplifying and paying attention can help reframe the clutter and relieve many pressures in your life. Staying on the career treadmill without a break only increases your stress levels and sense of being overwhelmed. I can't overemphasize the importance of taking time off for yourself—time to just rest and reflect *before* committing to your next steps. This can be a few days, weeks, or months. Some businesses and universities offer sabbaticals for the unique purpose of renewing their employees' creative energy and ideas. How could you create your own sabbatical? How much time would you need? How might you afford it? Who could help you plan it? When would you like to take it? I want you to look at your calendar. *"Sometime"* is not a date.

You also can't begin creating work you love until you get rid of some of the baggage you carry around with you. Let's start with your closets. Clean them out. Then clean out your car trunk and your garage. Throw out magazines and newspapers you haven't read in a month. Or find someone to help you. You can't read *everything* you want to. Ever. The backlog just accumulates and screams "read me!" along with all the other stuff that's yelling for your attention.

You'll be amazed at the freedom you feel when you get rid of stuff you don't need. Give it all to someone who will use it. Recycle it as gifts. Dump it. Donate magazines to your local library or hospital or nursing home. Notice extra "mind" space that shows up!

Trust me. This works. I love books, magazines, journals, and newsletters. I buy too many or borrow them by armloads from the library. Although I do read a lot, there is no way I could consume everything I want to. Periodically I put a halt to this compulsion. Julia Cameron in *The Artist's Way* recommends an exercise of not reading anything for one week. I tried it. The withdrawal felt similar to when I stopped smoking. Fortunately books aren't dangerous to my health. Nevertheless, I do take my own advice and throw out or donate those I don't read within a month. It feels great—until the next barrelful appears!

Try These:

1. Get rid of mind garbage. Throw out sweepstakes forms. They're time-wasters and hope-waxers. They seduce you into subscribing to yet another magazine that you don't have

time to read. Don't open unsolicited catalogs. What you don't see, you won't need.

2. Go on a news and talk-show diet. These programs clutter your mind-waves. Try not reading or listening to them for one day. Then another. Notice the extra creative thought-time that's suddenly available.

3. Create a ritual. Write down all the bad jobs you've had. State what you hated about them. If you didn't like or respect your managers or some of the people you worked with, write about that—what they were like, how they treated you, what you would have liked to have said to them but didn't. If what you hated was the location or the low salary or benefits or the hours or the stress, write about those too. Put it all down on paper. Write 40 pages. If that isn't enough, write 40 more. Read them over. Write more. Read them again. And again. Read them until you are tired of them. Then burn them. Watch the words and the anger go up in flame. They are over. In the past.

It's time to begin.

2

Create Safety

⨝⨝⨝

We have limited control, we only have choices.

When we feel safe, we can be truly creative and productive. When we're not, we are in survival mode and spend our time and energy licking our wounds.

Create Your Own Security in an Ever-Changing World

There is no such thing as job security. Create "work" security.

Please note:

- A young man or woman graduating from college today can expect six to ten job changes in his or her career.
- Every job you have should prepare you for the next one somewhere else—even if you choose to stay where you are now.
- You and your employer hire each other. They hire you for the skills, experience, and potential you bring. You hire them for the contribution you can make, the skills, knowledge, and experience you can gain as well as the paycheck. If you don't, you are committing career suicide.
- Working for someone else lulls us into a sense of "being taken care of." It is very seductive.
- "The average search time for a job is now under three months. Ironically, downsizing may be helping men and women find employment. Companies hire people more easily when they know they're not making a 30-year commitment."[5]
- Work is what you know *and* who you know. Some things never change.

Let's face it. There's no such thing as job security anymore. The headlines scream of layoffs, downsizing, mergers, and plant closings. We are in the middle of a major economic transition not experienced since we changed from an agricultural economy to an industrial one. *Weekends, retirement, benefits,* and *entitlements* were new concepts then. Today they are fast becoming things of the past. We no longer depend on a labor force that is located within our geographic borders. We don't know what tomorrow will look like, and we certainly don't know what *work-ing* will mean. And not knowing makes us *very* uncomfortable.

The truth is that we are all self-employed whether we receive paychecks or are in business for ourselves. The only security we have comes from doing work that supports us and our potential growth both inside and outside of the company that employs us. But how do we know if there will be a market for our skills in 5 to 10 years? How do we keep up? "I know I'm supposed to network, join organizations, be active, read professional journals," one software engineer recently told me. "But I'm already working 60 hours a week and so is everyone around me! I barely have time for a *life!*"

The paradigm is shifting. Many men and women, once caught in the never-ending spiral of climbing the career ladder to higher income, increased stress, less time for themselves and their families are crying, "Halt! Enough! I want a better life. A simpler one with meaningful work and friends and time to smell the roses." More and more people are starting their own businesses. Many are working from home or telecommuting. Networking and professional groups are providing the social communities once available only from corporations.

Pain, confusion, fear, and worry usually accompany any major change. Creating safety in the midst of insecurity begins at the personal level. *Yours.*

Try These:

1. Consider yourself an entrepreneur. Tell yourself you are contracting with your present or next place of work for a limited period—maybe three or five years, and you'll revisit this contract at the end of this time to see if it's beneficial for both you and the company to continue working together.

2. Write down what you want to *learn* from your current work. Will you learn that on the job or in training? Will this training be inside or outside the firm you are with? Who will pay for it? (Not who *should* but who *will*.)

3. Ask yourself what security means to you. Which items on the following list do you have control over? Which ones can you take steps toward to ensure that you have them in your life?

ᶜPredictability+	Money in the bank+	ᶜLifetime employment+
Being loved +	Good weather	A robust economy
ᶜGood health +	ᶜBelonging+	ᶜPeople I can count on +
ᶜIndependence+	ᶜFreedom to do	ᶜIntimacy/trust +
ᵃAutonomy +	as I choose +	ᶜHonesty +
ᵃFree choice+	ᶜInner peace+	ᶜPraise/acceptance +
ᵃRecognition/	ᵃPhysical/emotional	ᵃFriends/family +
belonging +	strength +	Own home +
ᶜLove +	ᵃPhysical safety/	ᵃAn accepting
Financial +	well-being +	environment +
independence	Other_____	Other

C — MUCH   a — SOME   + CAN TAKE STEPS TO ENSURE

Find Safety Where You Need It

Many people stay in unsatisfactory careers and relationships because they feel safer doing what they know, even if it's painful, rather than venturing into the unknown. They may become so overwhelmed by the prospect of what might happen if they were to do something different that they can't even begin. Their primary motivation is the desire to avoid pain or fear and to maintain their comfort and safety as they know it.

Others are motivated by risk and change or by freedom or solitude, while still others move toward the stability of being surrounded by lots of people. There are many people for whom safety means money in the bank and a firm social network. Others prefer to have nothing and no one to tie them down. How we define safety depends on our personal values as well as where we are in our lives. Our pattern for *managing* this safety through our many life changes is uniquely our own. For example, I am excited by change (as long as I see it as *good* change).

I see it as an opportunity to meet new people, stretch myself, learn about something new—a place, a company, a job. (That's fortunate considering my eclectic careers.) I also know that not everyone responds to change in the same way I do.

Look at the various changes you have gone through in your life. How did you react? For example, if you move to a new neighborhood or change jobs, do you feel a mixture of excitement and anxiety or only anxiety? Do you switch gears quickly? Do you need a lot of information before you make a new decision? Do you deliberate alone or do you ask others for input? Do you weigh pros and cons or do you jump right in? Do you look at change as an opportunity or with caution or dread? None of these ways of viewing change is intrinsically right or wrong.

My friend Tom's method is to take action at all costs. He will jump into the middle of the lake and start swimming across before he thinks about the water temperature. This has its pros and obvious cons. He will try something new (job, project, idea, etc.), succeed or fail, learn what works, try more of that, and continue this process until he ultimately gets the results he wants. Another friend, Carmen, will investigate, analyze the advantages and drawbacks, and then proceed. If her findings don't work, she'll try another tack—again using these methods— until she succeeds. Others will do endless research until they think they have enough information to take the first step. And sometimes they never feel ready to start. What are *your* patterns? And what do you need in order to take your next steps?

Try These:

This exercise involves an intuitive process. You have my permission to be silly.

1. Using pencils or crayons, draw a picture of yourself taking the first step toward something you want. Stick figures are

fine. Notice the feelings you have when you look at your picture.

I did this exercise before starting my first consulting business. At that time, I had been a headhunter for a number of years, and knew that I wanted to have my own consulting business. However, something was holding me back and I didn't know what it was. I drew a picture of myself at the edge of a cliff. The feeling I had was one of terror and that if I took one more step I would fall into the abyss below.

2. Now add something to your picture that would make you feel safe enough to take another step.

I drew pillows. A mountain of pillows from the bottom of the abyss to the top of the cliff so that if I fell I would be protected by their softness. I realized the pillows represented steps I needed to take to feel safe enough to begin. For me that meant finding information about (a) insurance policies and how much they would cost if I were on my own; (b) what I would need to do in order to start my business (have business cards and stationery printed, meet with an accountant, etc.); and (c) whom to contact in order to secure my first contract—all of which I did. I still use this pillow image whenever I get stuck and want to start something new. What image did you create?

3. What are your limitations? Do they involve money or know-how? If you are financially independent or have a partner who can help support you while you are starting out, you have fewer financial limitations than someone who doesn't. But if you don't, what steps can you start taking anyway?

4. What stops you from exploring? Frequently my clients have said, "If I do it and find it's not what I want, I'll be disappointed or embarrassed. I'm supposed to know it's right before I start." (How can they?) Or they are afraid of failing, losing their current friends, family, status quo, and even their current *un*happiness. For them being unhappy is more comfortable than trying something new.

5. What will you talk about if you aren't complaining about this job? Do you have a built-in agreement with your friends that "life is tough and then you die?"

Try This:

Switch your negative thinking to positive. Say to yourself:

"Life is perfect just the way it is. Everything that happens to me is happening for a reason. I'm doing exactly what I'm supposed to be doing right now. I'm just too close to it to understand the end result."

Take one step at a time. With every step you increase your own security.

Eliminate Negative, Critical People—or Train Them

Miracles do happen.

My mother used to be one of the world's most negative people. This became exceedingly clear to me the day I took her on a day trip to Ogunquit, a seaside village in Maine that she loves. There is a mile-long walk along the ocean cliffs as well as a congested tourist area called Perkins Cove, which has a lot of great art galleries and restaurants. As we approached the town I noticed a sign hanging from the porch of a large Victorian house that advertised a new restaurant. I said, "That looks interesting. Let's go there for lunch."

Mother immediately said, "Oh, you'll need reservations. We'll never get in." It was 10:30 in the morning. I said we could stop by after our walk.

As we drove on she asked, "Where are you going to park?"

"In Perkins Cove," I replied.

She said, "You'll never get a parking place. They're always crowded."

I said, "I always find parking spaces."

"Well, this is different," she warned me.

Now, Perkins Cove *is* always pretty jammed. But I spied someone just pulling out of a spot and I parked the car. We took our walk and went to the restaurant that I had suggested. There were only a few other diners and the food was excellent. When we left, we were crossing the street when Mother shouted, "Watch out!"

I stopped and asked, "What's wrong?"

"You could have tripped," she said. "There was a curb." I laughed. I was 40 years old.

In her way, my mother was still trying to protect me, to shield me from disappointment and potential harm. Her underlying belief was that the world was not a safe place. Her normal response was, "You can't do that," "It's too dangerous," "You need a different background, training, etc., to do that," or "You're going to do *what?!*" After I left my last job, burned out, and in physical and spiritual pain, I was feeling too vulnerable to listen to her worries about me—worries that would just mirror my own. I needed some time to heal and regroup.

Two weeks went by and I knew I couldn't delay seeing her any longer. She lives in a town about 20 miles away. No sooner did I enter the house than she began again: "I just don't understand it," she said. "What are you going to do?"

Some higher force came to my assistance this time. I said, "Mother, sit down. I want to tell you what I'm doing and why it's important and I ask that you just listen, please." I proceeded to tell her about my ideas for supporting people in their work. There were too many people in too much pain working in places that didn't nurture them. I had changed jobs and careers often enough to know this. My plan was to lead seminars and coach people by giving them information they didn't have so that they could have jobs they loved. I shared my vision for a book and a film that I wanted to do. I must have talked for 20 minutes without stopping. Her eyes didn't leave mine. When I stopped she said, "That's wonderful. People really need to hear this. Now I know why you've been so successful." I took another gulp of air and pushed on, "And what *I need from you is** your emotional support. I need you to tell me I'm doing the right thing, that you know I'll be successful because I don't always feel great and powerful but scared and worried. And I need you to say 'Yes, you can and you'll have hard days and yes, you can.'"

And from that day on my mother has been only supportive. If I am having a bad day, she listens and says, "Just keep at it. I know you'll do it. Look what you've done so far!" If she worries, she doesn't tell me. This was a major miracle in my life. And it opened up the space for a more intimate relationship with my mother. It's never too late!

Try These:

1. Stay away from negative, critical people. Run, don't walk. They only drain your energy. Choose friends who support and nurture you. If you can't avoid those who don't, be clear in your communication in what they can and cannot say to you. Honor your *self*!

2. The next time someone criticizes you or tells you you can't do something you want to do, (a) ask the person what he is basing that opinion on and (b) tell him what you want from him. Say the magic words, "What I need from you is _____." Then, if he can't respect your request, explain that you won't be able to be with him. (And don't smile.)

---

*Magic words

Do you want to please everyone or do you want to be happy?

Clarify your boundaries. And, no, not everyone will be happy about them. They don't have to be. It's your happiness you are working toward. However, if you don't insist on maintaining your boundaries, you will continue to attract people who will overstep them.

Help People Help You

The glass can be either half full or half empty. You can believe that others either want to help you or are out to get you. Whichever you choose, you will always be right. It will be easier for you if you choose the former. Being positive gives you more energy and vitality.

People want to help you succeed. Make this your mantra. It's actually true. When someone asks for *your* help, don't you want to help her? We all like to help others and give advice. It makes us feel good to contribute.

Your job is to provide those you ask with the right information so they *can* help you. It took me years of looking for jobs and feeling rejected to realize this. Finally I stopped "pushing the river in the opposite direction." I learned to determine what it was that *I* really wanted to do before I asked others to help me. And I needed to be selective about whom I asked.

Helping people help you begins with your accepting full responsibility for achieving your goals. It also means not asking for something you need from someone who can't give it to you. Asking for emotional support from someone who is uncomfortable with that level of intimacy will only disappoint you. Asking for a job from someone who can't give it to you will only make you both feel bad. And no one else can or should tell you what to do with your life.

Try Answering These:

1. Who do you feel safe with? Who can provide you with the emotional support you need? Who will respect your boundaries?
2. Who gives you support through entertainment, sports, or activities?
3. Who can provide financial assistance?
4. Who has helped you in your career(s) to date?
5. Who are others whom you trust and respect and who share similar values?
6. For your immediate goals, who can you ask for support and how can they help you?

How to Ask for What You Want

We usually give people permission to not give us what we want.

Who are you committed to?

What keeps most of us from asking for what we want—and getting it—is not knowing *how* to ask. Many of us are still unconsciously influenced by messages from our youth. We may live in fear that if we say something that reflects what we really want then (a) we will offend that person (be "in their face"), (b) they won't like us (who does she think *she* is?), (c) there won't be enough of something to go around (martyr's myth), and (d) it isn't safe. Some of these messages might have been necessary for our survival when we were younger. They aren't any longer.

My first consulting assignment (which led to a full-time position with projects, travel, and a large salary) came about because I *asked*. Remember the "pillows" information I needed to begin my first consulting business (page 29)? I tracked down the manager responsible for hiring contract recruiters at a company I wanted to work with. We finally met and talked for two hours. At the end of the meeting I said, "John, this has been a wonderful meeting. I've really enjoyed talking to you and I want to work with you."

"I've enjoyed it too," John replied.

"When can I start?" I asked.

He smiled, joining in the fun. "When would you *like* to start?"

It was Thursday and Monday was a holiday. "How about Tuesday?" I asked.

Taken aback, he said, "I don't know if I can get a purchase order."

I said, "Would you go find out?" He looked at me and said nothing. I said nothing too. He left the office. A few minutes passed and John returned with a signed purchase order. I started the following Tuesday.

Try These:

Here are some tips for helping people help you get what you want. Try them on. They may feel awkward at first. The longer you use them, the more comfortable you'll become because you'll see the results!

1. *Be clear in your own mind about what you want.* Write it down. Then commit to it 500 percent. Silence the inner critic that says it's not reasonable or possible. Remember the light bulb (page 14): You don't know what you don't know you don't know.

2. *If you don't ASK, you don't GET.* No one can read your mind. It is your responsibility to make sure you get the results you desire.

3. *Be direct.* Use words that say "I'm not kidding," such as *ask, request, propose.* When language is more formal it says "I'm serious." Even my kids didn't argue when I used these

words—they knew I meant business! If you must use soft words (such as *I'd like, would you, could you*, etc.), don't smile. Notice the difference in the feelings and intention of the stronger word choice below:

"I request that we meet this week to discuss my career," rather than

"I'd like to meet with you this week . . . ," or

"Would you meet with me this week . . . ?

4. *Set expectations.* Let people know what you want them to do and by when. Again, if you don't tell them, they will go on their own assumptions about what you want, which may not be what you meant. An example of this is misinterpreting the expression "ASAP" (as soon as possible). Does it mean within an hour? Next week? Yesterday? Immediately? When you get around to it?

How to Handle Unsafe Managers (or Anyone!)

Your real "job" is to make your boss successful. Your boss's job is to make you successful too. Without that neither of you will succeed.

Staying in jobs with nonsupportive managers can destroy your career.

First of all, most people I know haven't had too many good managers. Most managers aren't trained to manage (i.e., mentor, coach, support, lead) others. Most either fall into their role from a technical position or choose it as a way of climbing the career ladder. Although they may not admit it, they, like everyone else, are scared about their security and continued success. They are equally concerned about *their* managers, boards of directors, and customers.

This does not excuse inconsiderate, nonsupportive, or abusive behavior. Deadlines, pressures, and high stress can make anyone short-tempered *occasionally*. However, if you are experiencing continual harassment, insults, or embarrassments, you need to address them. Most miscommunication happens out of ignorance and not malice. Your goal is to train those with whom you don't feel safe. If this doesn't work, find another boss. Better sooner than later.

Gretchen worked in a fast-paced public relations firm in New York. It was her second job out of college and she had been there less than a year. She had been very excited to land this position. She loved the work, the clients, and her colleagues.

Her manager, Greg, was the owner of the company. Often he gave her projects to work on with sketchy instructions. Gretchen would document as best she could what Greg asked her to do. She checked in with him every two weeks with a progress report. Six weeks into one project, Greg stormed into her office shouting at her in front of her colleagues that she had "messed up." "How could you do that?" he yelled. "You should have done it another way." Gretchen, embarrassed and confused, followed him into his office to find out what she had done wrong. After all, she had kept him informed all along. He said she should have known what to do. Then he told her to get out of his office.

The next day, Greg came to the office as if nothing had happened. He gave Gretchen another assignment and left. She later confirmed with him the specifics of the project and the results he wanted. Three weeks later another abusive incident took place. This time Gretchen went to Greg's office and said that his reaction was unacceptable. She had kept him informed. She said that she was doing her job and wouldn't be yelled at—particularly in front of others. Did he want her to remain or look for another job? No, no, he assured her, he wanted her to stay. He told her she was making mountains out of mole hills.

It was clear to Gretchen that she was in a bind. This was her second job and she wanted to do well. The salary wasn't great, but she needed the experience. She was afraid if she left, it would look terrible on her record. Her parents had told her not to be a quitter. They said, "You need a job to find a job." But Gretchen also knew that the stress and harassment were eating away at her self-esteem. Her boss's style didn't work for her, and he wasn't listening to her concerns. She was afraid she wouldn't be able to present herself with confidence if she stayed there. She was scared but she decided to take the plunge and leave.

Luckily, Gretchen was an ace networker—a key skill for anyone in public relations. She did some temp work, talked to as many people as she could, went on dozens of interviews— some with companies she was hopeful about and others that mirrored the one she had just left. The latter she ruled out immediately. Her emotions were up and down between the interviews and the rejections. She didn't have much money left and was impatient to find work. After looking for four months, she found the job she wanted with a supportive company *and* with a salary increase of $5,000!

Too many people tolerate disrespectful behavior in the workplace. Don't be one of them. Your success begins and ends with you. You do have choices, although they may feel scarier than they actually are. Most people don't intend to be hurtful, they are just ignorant of their effect on others. If you happen to have someone like this as a boss, try training him or her or look for another manager.

Try This:

Try this for managing ignorant (uninformed) or abusive managers.

1. Request a private meeting.
2. Use the following script: "I need you to know that when you yell (or swear at me, ignore me, poke fun at me, grimace when I'm talking in meetings, use my computer to send

offensive memos, etc.), I find it insulting (harassing, embarrassing, etc.). It gets in the way of my work and it affects the whole team's performance."

Then be quiet. Wait for a response. He (or she) will probably apologize and say he hadn't intended to be offensive. Should he argue, dismiss, or negate what you said, say, "I hear you, and that is not my perception," and be quiet. Do not argue with him. You have said what you needed to.

3. If he continues this behavior despite your requests, and it is getting in the way of your productivity, you *must* take action. Document what happened and what he said. Be precise. Should you choose to report this to personnel or to his manager's boss, report just the facts. You probably won't be the first or last to file a complaint. Then request a transfer to another position or boss or look elsewhere. You cannot afford to stay working for a boss who doesn't support you. You will never succeed with such a person. Until you say "Halt!" you will continue to attract that kind of treatment from others.

Practice *Insurance* Listening

Communicating is complex.

Get feedback.

Just as we don't know what we don't know we don't know, we also don't know—*ever*—what is going on in someone else's mind. (We barely know what's going on in our own!) But very often we act as though we are mindreaders. We make assumptions about others' intent, what they really mean but aren't saying, even the hidden messages behind their looks or body language. (It might just be gas!)

In truth, we don't know what the other person is thinking, feeling, or saying because we generally aren't listening. Most people will deny this. But it's important to realize that most of the time we listen through our interpretations of who we think a person is. We ignore his or her background, culture, language differences, sex, upbringing, and physical and emotional makeup. But these are the things that influence the meanings behind each person's words and body language. We also ignore our own. Couple this with not paying full attention to what others are saying because we're thinking of other things at the same time and it's miraculous that we can communicate at all!

We speak at a rate of 80 to 120 words per minute. We think at a rate of 800 to 1,200 words per minute. That leaves a space of 700 to 1,100 words per minute that is rarely left unoccupied. That space is filled with thoughts of other things, e.g., what we're going to have for dinner, the project we have to complete, how we're impressing the other person, what we will say when he or she has finished talking, etc. In addition, we are not even conscious of our projections onto this person. For example, as you're talking to someone, that person may remind you of your mother, or an old boyfriend or girlfriend, or a person you once worked with who was a nightmare, etc. It takes total concentration and commitment to really *listen* to what someone is saying. In other words, it takes hard work!

To communicate effectively *you* must assume 100 percent of the responsibility for ensuring that you understand what the other person is saying. It is also up to *you* to make sure the other person understands what *you* are saying. Successful communication involves continually asking for feedback. We are all inundated with too much information, responsibilities, and pressures to be able to absorb what comes at us from all directions.

Try This:

1. *Observe what is being said.* What is the tone of voice? What emotions are involved? What is the person's body language telling you? (Remember that half of all communication is nonverbal.)

2. *Notice your interpretation of what is being communicated.* What do you *think* the person said? Of whom does he or she remind you?

3. *Ask for feedback on your interpretation.* You want to make sure you understand what the other person is saying to you. (Remember, we *all* listen through our prejudices.) It often helps to summarize: "Let me try to summarize what I heard. I want to make sure I've got it all," and "Is that what you meant?" Better to clear up any misunderstanding early rather than later when expectations have been set.

4. *Try this for one day:* Be with people in a way that you can honor them, their gifts, and their way of being. Know that this person in front of you (or on the phone, or on the Net) is very different from who you think he or she is. This person is *not* you. Every experience he or she has is different from any you have ever had. Even when you speak the same language, your understanding of the words is different. The only one ever to inhabit your body or mind is you. The only one to experience what you have experienced with your internal ear is you. The same is true for the other person. Even if the two of you were raised in the same family, have the same parents, went to the same schools, and ate the same food, you did not experience them in the same way. No one else is like you. Anywhere.

De-Stress Wherever You Are

Being overwhelmed, overworked, and stressed are not only major causes of fear and insecurity but are also the chief inhibitors to creative thinking, vitality, and life satisfaction, as well as peace of mind. We're working longer hours and having less time with our families, friends, and personal pursuits. The *quality* of your time, both at work and at home, is important. And the first step to attaining that quality is taking care of yourself and your own well-being. If you're stressed out, you aren't able to do your job, be creative, and support others.

Many of my clients complain of increasingly long hours. They feel they have no choice. Some are fearful of losing their jobs, even as they take over the work of displaced colleagues. Others want to be perceived as working as hard as their coworkers who stay late at the office or come in on weekends. There are others who enjoy what they are doing; they like the exciting energy of working hard with a group of people for a common goal. They just don't like being burned out or lacking time for the rest of their lives.

It is very difficult to keep your boundaries in an environment that doesn't value them. You may consider a different company that reflects more of the lifestyle you want. In a fast-paced, highly competitive, ever-changing marketplace, it is often the nature of that industry that drives the stress levels. And in some industries, high stress *is* the lifestyle!

You can also choose to make a major change and do something totally different. Whatever your choice, try these:

1. *Breathe.* Take a breath break to de-stress. Pay attention to your breath at periodic intervals during the day. You can do this when you are in meetings, in line in the supermarket, or in traffic. Notice your "out" breath. As you exhale say, "relax," and let all the tension leave your body. As you inhale say, "quiet." You can start by doing this for one to three minutes. Feel the difference.

2. *Notice your body.* Where are your shoulders? How do the muscles in your back feel? What about your stomach? Breathe into them. If the tension builds up, do something. Stretch. Stand up. Leave the room. Take a walk.

3. *Pay attention.* Listen to what others are saying. Observe how you are responding. If you find yourself getting upset, observe that too. You might want to write down your observations and feelings in a small notebook. That's all. Don't do anything about it. Just pay attention.

4. *Look for what's good about the situation.* For 24 hours, notice what is good about yourself, your job, and each person you speak with. We are so conditioned to criticize and find fault that we often overlook what is valuable. If a full day is too long, try it for 8 hours. Just try it!

5. *List all the things that bring you joy* and include at least one in your life. Daily!

Honor Your "Self"

"Nothing can bring you peace but yourself."
Ralph Waldo Emerson

Human beings weren't created to live at the pace we live at.

There has been much written about the connection of the body, mind, and soul. Many alternative health practices, such as meditation, vegetarian diets, acupuncture, hypnotherapy, etc., that were once considered New Age (and therefore less valid) have been adopted by doctors and psychologists worldwide. We have learned that when we ignore the connections between our body, mind, and soul and relentlessly push ourselves to be other than we are, we suffer either physically, emotionally, spiritually, or all three. At the rapid pace we live our lives, it is critically important for us to pay attention to who we are and what we really need to be healthy and vital.

I learned this the hard way as I drove along the road to success. Pinched nerves and muscle spasms spoke clearly when I ignored my body/soul needs. Today when I coach clients on their careers I ask them what they are doing to take care of themselves *right now.* Since they can't immediately change their environment, I ask that they think about what they can do in the present moment to increase their sense of well-being.

One of my clients, Joan, a senior consultant in an environmental firm, was unhappy with the amount of stress in her job.

She wanted more balance, but she knew she wasn't ready to make any major changes. I asked her what her office looked like. She said it was very functional and nothing was hung on the walls. I then asked her how she would like to *feel* at work if she had the balance she wanted. She said she wanted to feel the way she does when she's in church—quiet, centered, and at peace. I asked, "Where else do you have these feelings?"

Joan said, "When I'm in the mountains, in nature." We explored how she could bring something into her office that might elicit those feelings—a poster of a mountain scene, pictures of flowers, or even flowers themselves. She said she had thought of that but that she hated decorating and had little talent for it. She also thought her professional image might be at risk if she were to do this. I assured her that enlivening her office would only strengthen her image. Really powerful people celebrate all parts of themselves. I asked if any of her friends would be willing to do the decorating for her if she asked. Her face brightened. Of course, she had two friends who would be more than happy to help.

We then explored other ways she could bring balance into her daily activities. Everyone in the company ate lunch at their desks. Joan liked to walk at lunch but feared that doing this would make her appear a slacker. I suggested she ask others to walk *with* her and start a new trend. Joan started a lunchtime walking group and not only got more exercise and energy but also got to know her colleagues in the process! They just needed to be asked!

What you need is often what others need too.

By honoring yourself, you also honor others.

Try Answering These:

1. What does your body need? What does your soul need? If you are tired, how can you rest? If you need solitude, how can you make time for yourself?

2. If you are feeling stressed, whom can you talk to? Research shows that talking to a good friend or counselor is one of the best antidotes for managing upsets and keeping them from manifesting in your body later.

3. If beauty is important to you, how can you bring it into your life—daily?

4. What form of physical exercise could you do to take care of your body? How can you make time for it?

5. What about your spiritual side? What does spirituality mean to you? How can you bring that into your day-to-day activities?

Act As If the Universe Is Supporting You

"Ninety-eight percent of what I worried about never happened."

Mark Twain

We are given what we need, not always what we want.

When I look back over lists of goals I have had, I am amazed at how many of them came true. My clients tell me the same is true for them. We may not have reached our goals exactly when we wanted or in precisely the way we had imagined—but we did reach them.

When I was younger I had dreamed of being a teacher, an actress, an artist, a writer, and of having my own business. I also dreamed that it would be easy. Today I am teaching, speaking to large audiences, writing, painting, and I have my own business. But the paths to these dreams were not as I had envisioned nor am I doing them in exactly the way I had imagined. I had also dreamed of being in France. It was a fantasy supported by my love of the language and everything French. My last company sent me to France, Switzerland, and French-speaking Canada, as well as to Asia and across the United States.

My daughter, Sara, has had part-time jobs since she was fourteen. The summer between college and law school, when she was working as a waitress at a restaurant on Martha's Vineyard, an attorney came in and asked the owner if he knew someone who could do bookkeeping. The restaurant owner told Sara and she applied for the job. Sara's dream was to be an arbitrator—this lawyer's specialty. (Coincidence?) He became her mentor, gave her legal work to do, brought her to hearings, and introduced her to a wealth of contacts. She never did much bookkeeping.

There is much written about belief and the power behind our thoughts. Positive thoughts beget positive thoughts. You can reframe your life by focusing on the positive of all your experiences—including your limitations—how they strengthened you and what you learned from them.

> "[Have] thoughts so strong they act as beliefs, and beliefs strong enough to make things happen."
> Jack Hawley

Try These:

1. Think of times in your life when you have been supported in your goals as if by magic—when people, money, or resources just seemed to show up. Act as if that will happen again with your current desire. Expect the magic and move toward it.

2. What if you knew that one year from today you would have your dream (job, mate, home, goal, etc.) and that what you are doing now is preparation for that dream? And what if you knew that when you had attained your dream you would be totally consumed by it? How would you spend your time now?

3. Make a list of 10 or 20 goals you have. Then act as if they are going to happen. Act as if you are handing them over to a power greater than you. This power will take care of the details.

4. Read the story of the man and his boat on page 143.

Make your wish, let it go, and let the Universe take care of the details.

MOYERS: Do you ever have this sense when you are follow-
            ing your bliss, as I have at moments, of being
            helped by hidden hands?

CAMPBELL: All the time. It is miraculous. I even have a super-
            stition that has grown on me as the result of invis-
            ible hands coming all the time—namely, that if you
            do follow your bliss, you put yourself on a kind of
            track that has been there all the while, waiting for
            you, and the life that you ought to be living is the
            one you are living. When you can see that, you
            begin to meet people who are in the field of your
            bliss, and they open the doors to you. I say, follow
            your bliss and don't be afraid, and doors will open
            where you didn't know they were going to be.

                        Joseph Campbell and Bill
                        Moyers, *The Power of Myth*[6]

3

Increase Your Creativity

—∞∞∞—

"Imagination is more important than knowledge."

Albert Einstein

"Creativity is harnessing universality and making it flow through your eyes."

Peter Koestenbaum

Shelve Your Inner Critic

The only difference between a creative person and a noncreative one is in the saying so.

We live in a constantly changing marketplace where we seem to have an insatiable appetite for new services, products, crafts, and art forms. A large percentage of the products and services that will be available in the next ten years haven't even been invented yet. It's through our unique creativity and imagination that we can tap into special ways to use our gifts and passions to support the needs of the new millennium. As we learn to expand our creative thinking, we expand our ability to develop new solutions, ideas, and ways of living.

A creative person—artist, writer, entrepreneur, thinker—will describe herself as creative and therefore look for imaginative ways of approaching problems and finding solutions. Conversely, someone who describes herself as noncreative will stick with the tried and true. Such a person has devised a structure to define herself that feels safer than venturing into the unknown. And that person has had lots of support and agreement from others in the process. She may not realize that her perceived safety net may actually be the *riskiest* place to stay.

Everyone is imaginative and creative—just look at children under the age of six at play. (And we were all once children!) They build fantastic structures out of any material, make up stories and imaginary friends, explore and draw with abandon, and take great pride in what they produce or find! At least they do until someone tells them that they shouldn't or that their creation or idea needs to be a certain way, is wrong, or silly. That usually happens when they go to school.

Most of us weren't trained to be creative. We were trained to be analytical, logical, detail-oriented, judgmental, and reasonable. Creativity comes out of unreasonableness. It comes out of imagination, intuition, humor, vision, music, and nonjudgment. For many, being creative was shut down in the busy-ness of growing up, achieving, earning, and managing everyday living. We may have protected that part of ourselves as we tried to fit in, please others, and survive. It didn't disappear; it was just hiding until it felt safe enough to come out.

The first step to awakening creativity is to shelve the Inner Critic (IC). Your IC is that voice inside your head that is continually lecturing, criticizing, blaming, and shaming. It judges you and everyone around you. It whispers loudly and insistently. "Who do you think *you* are?" "You see, you did it again!" "You're not _____ enough." "They'll think you're foolish if you say that." "That'll never work." "What a stupid idea." "We tried that one before." "There's no market for it." "How could anyone think that?" "Who do they think *they* are?" "They aren't the type of people I want to be with." It's the voice of your parent, grandparent, teacher, clergyman, boss, etc. And if you didn't have one that sounded like that, you made one up anyway.

Your IC is your oldest, most constant companion. It is also your enemy. It keeps you from accepting your uniqueness and moving forward. It keeps you stuck in the same old routines and puts the brakes on your imagination and creativity. You can't get rid of your IC entirely, but you can weaken its power by shaking hands with it and shelving it temporarily.

Try These:

1. When your IC rears its head, tell it that you appreciate its input and you are putting it on the shelf in the closet and closing the door. You will get back to it at _____. (Give it a specific time or it won't stop chattering. At the designated time you can resume the conversation if it is still interested.)
2. Have a dialogue with your IC in your journal. This is an excellent way to sort through problems.

Example:

ME: I'm writing a book.

IC :   You're kidding! *You* can't write a book! Who do you think you *are*? Remember Ms. Terry's eleventh grade English class? You got a C! It was the first C you ever had because you weren't as good a writer as everyone else. Remember? And your parents were so mad they sent you to summer school. With nuns!

ME: Yes, I remember. And that was the first time I was taught grammar well enough to understand it!

IC: Yeah, but you haven't even written a story!

ME: I'm not writing fiction! I've written newsletters and articles that lots of people liked.

IC: What do *they* know?

ME: Many of the people who sent me notes were writers and marketing people.

IC: Yeah, but . . .

ME: I'm not going to continue listening to you right now. I hear you and you are annoying. I'm putting you in the closet. I'll get back to you tomorrow morning at 10:00.

Trust me. Shelving *your* IC will feel great!

Trust Your Intuition

"The intellect has little to do on the road to discovery. There comes a leap in consciousness, call it intuition or what you will, and the solution comes to you and you don't know how or why."
Albert Einstein

In this jumbled time of accelerated change, if you can't trust your intuition, what can you trust?

Pray, wait, take time to listen to the voice within. And follow that.

The mind/body connection, once thought revolutionary, has gone mainstream. Intuitive insight has gained respect even in boardrooms. Ask a CEO how he finally resolved a difficult problem, he'll probably say, "After reviewing all the facts, I went with my gut."

I grew up doubting myself. I believed that others (males in particular) had the answers and were smarter, more experienced, older, wiser. They said they knew best, and I believed them. When I found myself on my own, I needed to provide a safe home for my children, find work, manage day-to-day crises, and succeed without training. I had to listen to my gut. I was in survival mode. I didn't have any role models and was too busy to find them.

I learned that my instincts were usually correct about people and jobs. The more I paid attention to my senses the more they proved good advisers. My old tapes continued to argue with my gut so I didn't always follow its advice. I didn't think I had any choice and my body paid for it. When my body yelled loudly enough, I listened.

This gut feeling, inner knowing, God, Spirit, or intuition is some mysterious insight that just *happens*. You know when you hear it, but you don't know how you know. New ideas, inspiration, real understanding, inventive thinking, and creativity come from this magical place. It comes from your essence when you are relaxed, unaware, doing something else or nothing at all. It speaks to you through your body, your senses, and your own uncensored thoughts. The more you pay attention to what it is telling you, the more you will trust it. If you are in comfort or discomfort, that is your intuition speaking. You know everything you need to know right now. You just forgot because of all the noise.

We humans constantly talk to ourselves. This leaves little space for creative thought. Creativity comes out of nothingness, the gap between the thoughts. We fill ourselves with current and past knowledge, old tapes and messages, and limited thinking. We tell ourselves we've got it figured out, then drive ourselves nuts with projecting, analyzing, fearing, and worrying.

I like the story of the professor who taught Buddhism and visited a Zen monk to learn more. As was customary, the monk offered him tea. The professor expounded on what he knew about Buddhism while the monk poured the tea. He continued talking as the monk continued pouring. The liquid filled the cup and spilled over onto the professor's pants. The professor cried out, "There's no more room! The tea is overflowing the cup!" The monk stopped and said, "Just like you. You have so much in your head, there is no room for any more."

Trusting your intuition takes practice.

Try These:

1. *Listen to your body.* Notice your comfort levels when you are making minidecisions such as what you want to eat, what you want to wear, who you like being with, and which parts of your job you like most. Listen to what your body is saying whether or not you choose to do what it is telling you. Don't judge, just observe.

2. *Draw a mind map.* One technique is to ask a question and jot down whatever image or word comes to you on a blank piece of paper. From this image, add other thoughts. Whichever idea produces in you a feeling of "aha," circle it; it is giving you more information. The image doesn't need to make sense. Don't judge it, just write it down. If you don't understand the meaning of the words or symbols, ask your intuition for more information—and let go of the need to know. Trust that the answers will come to you in time. You

may find the answer in a book you are reading or in something someone says. Then notice what shows up during the day or in your dreams. Jot this down in a small notebook that you carry with you or on a pad of paper you keep near your bed. (It is important to turn off your IC for this exercise.)

3. *Do an intuitive drawing.* Remember when you were a kid and you would lie on your back and look up at the sky and find pictures in the clouds? This is a similar game. Let your pencil, pen, or crayons move around a large blank piece of paper. Make marks where your body/mind tells you to. Draw them bold or faint. You can scribble, use your non-dominant hand, or close your eyes. When you have the faintest thought to use a different material, that is your inner voice speaking. Pick up the new material. Never mind whether your drawing makes sense. No judging allowed. Give yourself 10 minutes for this drawing. Then do another. Draw how you feel. Draw your impression of your boss, job, colleagues, friends, etc. Put the drawings on the wall and look at them. Look at the shapes. What do you see? How do you feel when you look at the shapes?

4. *Guess.* Start making predictions. When the phone rings, guess who is on the other end. Before you check your answering device, guess how many calls will be waiting. Or if you are choosing a line at the grocery store, guess which one will go fastest. Sometimes you will guess the right one, and sometimes you won't. As you practice, notice how you *feel* when you guess correctly. (And don't judge yourself wrong when you don't guess correctly. This is a *game*, remember.)

The answer is showing itself to you. You just need to receive it. If you have a yearning to do something, pay attention. That is your inner self speaking. If you are drawn to a certain country, visit it. If you are constantly buying art supplies, use them and don't judge the results. You don't become fluent in a language in just one day.

They [some people] become so locked into this way of thinking [legalistic, scientific] that it often takes something as extreme as a major illness to shake the current paradigm. Only when thus shaken can they make the leap to faith. It's always a leap into the void because at those times there's simply no more "proof" to prop ourselves against. The point is that sooner or later we have to make the leap—we have to let go of understandable logic and make the big step beyond. And when that leap is made, the fall is usually straight up, toward Spirit.

There's quietness and serenity at these heights, closer to Spirit. This is the place of certainty, of moments of faith so high we merge with truth. This is where something at our core whispers "yes . . . yes" with full confidence. It brings the bounty of clarity, of seeing from higher self, the boon of being sure. This is when it all makes sense, when everything fits, when we know it's all happening as it is meant to, when we really understand that it is all okay.

This level of faith does not lead to stupid obedience to worldly level things or people. It's the exact opposite of that. This is the flowering of our own internal "evidence," the blooming of our own "proof," the creation of our own "authority."

> Jack Hawley, *Reawakening the Spirit of Work*[7]

Be Curious, Not Smart

"In the beginner's mind there are many possibilities, but in the expert's there are few."

> Shunryu Suzuki, *Zen Mind, Beginner's Mind*

"Everything that can be invented has been invented."
>Charles H. Duell, Commissioner,
>U.S. Office of Patents, 1899

"The horse is here to stay, but the automobile is only a novelty—a fad."
>President of the Michigan
>Savings Bank advising Henry
>Ford's lawyer not to invest in the
>Ford Motor Company

"Heavier than air flying machines are impossible."
>Lord Kelvin, 1895

"Who the hell wants to hear actors talk?"
>Harry Warner, president of
>Warner Brothers Pictures, 1927

"Video won't be able to hold on to any market it captures after the first six months. People will soon get tired of staring at a plywood box every night."
>Daryl F. Zanuck, head of 20th
>Century Fox movie studio,
>commenting on television, 1946

"I think there is a world market for maybe five computers."
>Thomas Watson, chairman of
>IBM, 1943

"There is no reason for any individuals to have a computer in their home."
>Ken Olsen, president, chairman,
>and founder of Digital
>Equipment Corp., 1977

Most of us believe we have to have the answers. We value logical thinking, scientific reasoning, research, analytical skills, appropriate and grown-up behavior. We esteem being in control, taking action, making money, and being social. Anything that doesn't support these behaviors and attributes is declared nice but unimportant.

Consequently we don't give our imaginations—and spirits—the space they need to grow. We are endlessly goal-driven from the time we are children. When you were in grade school, adults probably asked you what you were going to be *when* you grew up. As you got older the questions changed to what courses you were going to take *after* your vacation, what colleges you were applying to *when* you finished high school, which graduate school, what job, what career *path*, what *plans*. The constant refrain became: "What are you going to do next?!"

We are like continually spinning tops—never stopping until we wear ourselves out. Sometimes getting sick and being forced to stay in bed is the only rest we get!

Time to do nothing is frowned upon. How many people would feel comfortable sitting and thinking for long periods without actually doing something at work? To be painting or drawing or reading poetry would appear frivolous. Although it is well known that the greatest insights and creations have come when least expected, when the mind is relaxed, we are programmed to take action at all costs.

As we are creating something new, something original, we can't know what this will be until it comes to us. Finding your niche is similar. It grows out of *not knowing* what the answer is. It comes from being curious and exploring the questions. It comes from paying attention to *now*.

"Develop an interest in life as you see it; in people, things, literature, music—the world is so rich, simply throbbing with rich treasures, beautiful souls, and interesting people. Forget yourself."
Henry Miller

Try These:

1. *Look at the world as if from a child's eyes.* When you are driving on a familiar street, look at the neighborhood as if you are seeing it for the first time—as if you are visiting a foreign country and observing how people live. Notice the size of their houses. Do they have gardens? What types of trees and greenery do you see? Do this for an hour, a day, a week.

2. *Try the same thing with people you know.* Pretend that you are meeting them for the first time and that they come from a different culture (which they do). You will listen to them differently. What are they really like?

3. *Practice open-minded curiosity.* Approach a work or personal problem as an observer: "Hmm, let's see what this one is about. What can I learn here? Maybe I'll discover something new."

4. *Turn off your judgment switch for one 24-hour period.* Then another.

Embrace Failure

"Eighteen publishers turned down Richard Bach's 10,000-word story about a soaring seagull before Macmillan finally published it in 1970. By 1975, *Jonathan Livingston Seagull* had sold more than seven million copies in the U.S. alone.

"Walt Disney was fired by a newspaper for lacking ideas. He also went bankrupt several times before he built Disneyland.

"Leo Tolstoy, author of *War and Peace*, flunked out of college. He was described as both unable and unwilling to learn.

"Henry Ford failed and went broke five times before he finally succeeded."

Jack Canfield and Mark Hansen,
Chicken Soup for the Soul[8]

Success depends on being willing to fail—often.

We have all heard the story of Thomas Edison's many attempts to invent the light bulb. "Mr. Edison," someone asked him, "is it true that you had over 10,000 failures while trying to invent the light bulb?" "Young man," said Tom, "those weren't failures. Those were practice tests. I learned what *not* to do from each of them."

One of the silliest messages I grew up with was, "If you can't do it right, don't do it at all!" Why not? Being willing to fail opens up myriad opportunities, relationships, and experiences. So why do many people try to avoid failing at all costs? They are afraid that if they fail, they will look foolish, be embarrassed, or feel ashamed. Then people won't like or respect them and their life will be over! Is this really true or just another myth? Who *said* you had to have the perfect answer/job/skill/mate on the first try?

Failure means not reaching the goal you have set for a specific time period.

Extend your time period. Or reassess your goal.

You may be failing because you are on the wrong path. You may be following someone else's desires and not pursuing your own. You will never be motivated by what you don't want.

"Picasso created over 20,000 works of art, most of which were considered worthless. But he learned and sharpened his technique from each try."

Ray Anthony and Malcom
Kushner, *High Octane Selling*

"I think and think for months and years. Ninety-nine times, the conclusion is false. The hundredth time I am right."

Albert Einstein

Try These:

1. List how some of your failures have opened doors to new opportunities, relationships, or new knowledge. What have you gained from them?
2. Try doing something that you haven't done before. Write a poem or a story, draw a picture, create an object out of odds and ends. Commit to failing at it 30 times. Then 30 more until you like what you have created.
3. Write a paragraph or two about what you would do if you knew you couldn't fail.

Go "Outside the Box"

A baby elephant is trained not to run away by tying it to a post with a strong rope. When it is an adult, it needs only a thin cord.

When I started my first consulting assignment for a large multinational company years ago, I didn't know what I wasn't supposed to do or whom I shouldn't speak to. I hadn't grown up there. My previous business experience had been in sales with start-ups and smaller companies. I had read somewhere that to reach the decision maker, you should start at the top. So I always called the president. She and her secretary were usually helpful. Again, I didn't know there was a correct way in this organization. I thought my job was to get things done. So if one person or department couldn't help me, I'd go to another until I found someone who would. Sometimes I called the vice presidents. They were helpful too! (Ignorance sometimes works to our advantage!) When the management of one of the groups I was working with offered me a job I couldn't refuse, I thought they were kidding. I didn't fit their job descriptions, which generally required a technical background. I asked them why they wanted me. They said, "You don't understand what the word *no* means and you get things done." My maverick behavior had resulted in a great full-time job!

We live inside scatomas or blind spots to what we don't know. When the Spanish galleons appeared on the horizon coming to the Americas, the Indians weren't alarmed because they didn't "see" them. They had never seen a vessel of that size; it was outside of their comprehension. The rest is history.

In the puzzle on page 65, connect the nine dots with four straight lines without taking your pen off the paper. (The answer is on page 66.)

If you struggled with this puzzle (even if you have done it before), you are experiencing scatomas or blind spots. These blind spots are what we don't see because of habitual thinking, seeing, and doing. They are similar to the blind spots that keep us from seeing options within our careers.

To break up your scatomas and jump-start your creative engines, try some things you don't ordinarily do (without judgments).

Example:
1. Take a different route to work.
2. Listen to music you don't ordinarily listen to.
3. Explore a new place.
4. Eat food you've never tried.

5. Go to a junkyard, hardware store, toy store, art store. See what you are attracted to. Could any of the stuff liven up your work or home environment? Could it be useful or fun?
6. State a goal and list some incredible ways of reaching it. Then make the goal bigger.
7. Look at a problem through a child's eyes.
8. Pretend you are an alien from another planet. What would you think about the problem then?
9. Be the problem. Rather than trying to figure out the answer, pretend you are the problem.
10. Write a letter to Congress.

We are unaware of our power.

Look for What's Positive and Useful

If you are like most people, you have been conditioned to focus on negatives. Unfortunately, finding fault and concentrating on bad news or what's wrong clogs your creative energy. You listen to or read the news that reports the tragic events of the day. At work you talk about what (and who) needs to be fixed (broken or not). People often believe that being critical means they are smarter, more discerning, better judges. If someone comes up with a new idea, the usual response is why it *won't* work. It's no wonder we have trouble coming up with alternative creative approaches! Who wants to get shot down?

SWITCH! It's time to make a change. Look for the positives. Be open to new ideas without judgment.

Try These:

1. What is positive and useful about working in this job? (Even if you hate it.) What is positive about your boss and your coworkers?

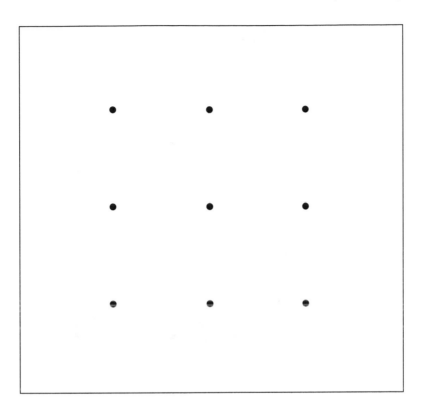

2. What is positive and useful about leaving your job?
3. What is positive and useful about a specific idea or person? Choose any idea or person that you encounter over the course of the day. Be on the lookout for them. You don't have to say anything; just observe.
4. What is positive and useful about liking to _____? Fill in whatever skill, interest, or personality trait you have. Then list as many ideas as you can. Be outrageous!

Example:

What is positive and useful about liking to read?

1. I can learn about anything that interests me.
2. I find new information and ideas that I might be able to use sometime.

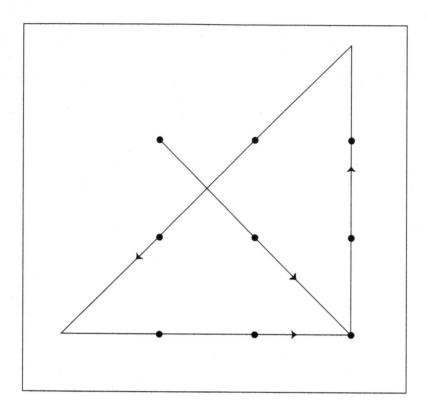

3. There are lots of experts I can learn from.
4. I learn to improve my writing by reading books by good writers.
5. I can talk to others who are interested in the same subjects.
6. I can contact authors through their publishers.
7. I can teach others what I read about.
8. I can speak about what I read.
9. I can write about what I read.
10. I can give workshops.
11. I can publish a newsletter, give summaries of what I've read, and advertise it on the Internet.
12. I can start a lending library or a used-book store with my books.

13. I can donate my books to libraries or give them as gifts.
14. I can use my books as decoration or as legs for a glass-top coffee table.
15. I can cut out articles from my magazines and send them to clients or use them in a collage.
16. I can form a book club specializing in my interests.
17. I can offer my services as a reader to nursing homes, day care centers, after-school programs, libraries, English-as-a-second-language programs, or busy executives by summarizing and taping news they are interested in and sending it to them daily via Federal Express.
18. I can (your ideas).

Brainstorm

A powerful way to come up with creative ideas is to invite friends and colleagues (and even strangers) to help you. The dynamic synergy of the group will cause the creation of new thoughts that you couldn't come up with on your own. The best ideas may come at the end of the brainstorming session or after everyone has gone home.

To start a brainstorming session, gather three or more people and tell them what you are trying to accomplish. Then name one to two obstacles that are keeping you from getting there (e.g., you don't know how; you don't have the money; your boss, partner, or kids won't let you). Have paper and pencil ready, be quiet, and just listen and write.

Rules of Brainstorming

For the Person Receiving Ideas Avoid saying "That's a good idea," "That's dumb," "I don't think so," or "I've already done that and it doesn't work." Don't make a face, raise your eyebrows, or roll your eyes in pleasure or disdain. It will make the person speaking feel judged or stupid and will also stop *everyone's* creative energy and ideas. Just write down what is said. Often it is the seemingly silliest ideas that give us what we need.

For the Person(s) Giving Ideas Don't say "Did you do . . . ," "You should . . . ," or "Have you thought of . . . ?" All of these will imply that the person is stupid for not having done or thought of them before and will stop his creative energy and attention. Just give ideas with action verbs, e.g., "Go to . . . ," "Call . . . ," "Write to . . . ," etc. Also while brainstorming, think about people you know. Which ones might be good resources who could help your friend?

For further ideas on brainstorming, see Chapter 7.

Try These:

Use the following for brainstorming exercise either with a group or by yourself:

Remember the earlier exercises where you identified your top three to five gifts, skills, interests, and qualities? In the following exercise you will bring them together. For example, here is what I did:

1. On a clean sheet of paper, list your gifts/skills, interests, and qualities in this format:

Gifts/Skills	Interests	Qualities
Writing	Personal development	Visibility
Coaching	Europe	Autonomy
Teaching	Art	Variety
Interviewing	International cultures	Creativity

2. Start brainstorming using your interests and linking them with your gifts/skills that you want to use and expand now.

Example:

Brainstorming Session 1 Interest: Personal development (which includes health, psychology, philosophy, fitness, spirituality, creativity, personal empowerment, lifestyles, etc.)

My *gifts/skills* (that I want to use and increase now) are:

Writing	Coaching	Teaching	Interviewing
MAYBE I COULD:			
work for health or fitness magazines	coach people on the phone	teach people how to do work they love	interview self-help gurus
write a newsletter and give tips from all books I've read	set up interactive coaching sessions on the Internet	lead creativity seminars in Europe	have my own radio talk show
write about spiritual practices around the world		lead intuition seminars on cruise ships	be a journalist
		teach a weekly stress relief class on TV	

3. Now pick another interest and link it with the same gifts/skills as above. Continue this brainstorm session by linking the rest of your interests with your gifts/skills.
4. Now brainstorm by linking an important quality with your interests.

Example:

Brainstorming Session 2 Quality: Autonomy/having own business

My *interests* (that I want to use now) are:

Europe	Art	International Cultures
MAYBE I COULD:		
publish a magazine about European life	write about intuitive drawing	write about Japanese health rituals
open a bed and breakfast in England	be an art critic	work for the United Nations
	sell my paintings	

Finish this brainstorm session by linking the rest of your qualities with your interests.

Do Yoga, Take a Walk

New Age stuff is just Old Age stuff recycled.

Over the years I have found that physical movement and yoga are the best antidotes for inertia, creative blocks, "same old" thinking, and stress. Instead of struggling to "figure it out," I've learned to stretch, breathe, and take a walk—in nature whenever possible. I leave my desk, office, house (as well as my credit cards and checkbook) and find trees, flowers, grass, and sunlight. I try to look at them as if for the first time.

Yoga has become a popular alternative to the frenetic activity of aerobic exercise. Yoga is meditation in motion. It is an ancient Indian discipline made up of a series of gentle movements and postures (held positions) that release endorphins (the "bliss" hormones) and rid the body of muscle tensions. Endorphins create a sense of well-being and centeredness. Practicing yoga helps you to listen with your whole body, not just your ears. I credit yoga with saving my sanity many times. It has helped me make major changes (e.g., leave toxic relationships—both personal and work-related), overcome addictions (smoking and junk food), and manage stress.

Try These:

1. Take a walk at lunchtime. Commit to walking at least 30 minutes a day.
2. Enroll in a yoga class at your local YMCA or adult education program. Although there are videos that can get you started, I recommend a class with an accomplished teacher to guide you. You will notice the difference in your body after the first class.

If you can't or don't want to do yoga or take a walk, choose something else. Run; play tennis, golf, or other sports; or swim. Do anything that will get you moving!

Practice Silence—Meditate

"Meditation is not something different from daily life. It is total attention. 'Attention' implies to attend, that is to listen, hear, see, with all the totality of your being, with your body, with your nerves, with your eyes, with your ears, with your mind, with your heart, completely."

> J. Krishnamurti,
> *The Flight of the Eagle*

"Creativity comes out of nothingness."
> Gertrude Stein

Meditation is the best way I know to carve out a little oasis of silence against the din of everyday living. The purpose of meditation is to achieve heightened awareness. It quiets the mind (and body) and allows for fresh insights, understanding, and creativity.

I started meditating after being introduced to yoga in my early twenties. It gave me a new way of being that I hadn't experienced before—quieter, more relaxed, and centered. It quickly became a part of my life. I noticed that the effects of meditation were cumulative—the more consistently I meditated, the more relaxed and intuitive I became.

Try This:

There are many ways to meditate. Here is one I recommend:

1. Choose a time each morning and each evening when you will have 15 to 20 minutes of undisturbed time. You may want to negotiate this time with your family or housemates or get up 20 minutes earlier. If you are new to meditating, start with 10 minutes. Install an answering device or service on your phone and turn the ringer off. It's important to get rid of distractions. (When I was raising my kids I would meditate when I came home from work before preparing dinner. If I didn't meditate, I would be too grumpy and *they* would send *me* to my room!)
2. Sit in a chair with your back straight and your feet flat on the ground or on a foot rest. It is important that your back be straight and your legs uncrossed. If you are comfortable sitting cross-legged on the floor, that is fine too, but not necessary.
3. Place your hands palm-down on your lap.
4. Close your mouth and breathe through your nose.
5. Close your eyes.

6. Notice where your shoulders are and lower them. Notice any tension in any part of your body, and as you breathe repeat silently the word *relax* into that tension.
7. Notice your breath as you inhale and exhale. Notice the air coming into your nostrils and throat as you inhale. Feel it leaving as you exhale. As you inhale, say to yourself, "I breathe in." As you exhale, say to yourself, "I am quiet."

If you are like most of us, you will think you are doing it wrong. Your mind will wander in whatever form of meditation you choose. With practice, it will wander less. Nevertheless, you may have judgments about how well or how poorly you are meditating. One experience may feel better (more relaxed, more blissful, lighter) than another. However, since the purpose of meditation is heightened awareness, to meditate is to continually bring your mind back to the focus. If there are sounds of traffic or birds or voices, they too are part of the process. To meditate means to be in the present moment.

"Breathing in I calm my mind and body
Breathing out I smile
Breathing in I dwell in the moment
This is the only moment"

Thich Nhat Hanh

Play Baroque Music

When you are relaxed, creativity happens.

When I'm having writer's (or artist's) block, I play Baroque music (e.g., Bach) or Gregorian chants. I've heard that the repetitive slow rhythm of this style of music has a calming effect on the central nervous system, thereby allowing for increased creativity. With this soothing sound in the background, I am able to write or draw more easily. The words or lines seem to flow on their own.

Consult a Psychic

Try a different perspective.

Psychic or intuitive counselors can provide you with answers that your logical mind can't. You would be surprised by how many of your friends and colleagues include annual visits to their favorite soothsayer as part of their wellness programs. They leave these sessions energized and looking at their lives and problems in a different light.

Visiting psychics, astrologers; playing Runes; or reading the I Ching, Medicine Cards, the Tarot, and other similar devination tools can help you jump-start the intuitive and creative right side of your brain. The magic comes from how you *apply* what you hear or read. Rather than interpret the information literally, ask yourself what it might symbolize in your life. What clues is it triggering for you? You can even make up your own fortune-telling system.

Try This:

1. Open a dictionary, magazine, or newspaper.
2. Ask it a question such as "What should I do next?" or "How else can I approach this?"
3. Close your eyes and put your finger on a word at random.
4. Ask yourself how this word applies to your question. Play with it. Mindmap it. Write a verse, story, or fairy tale using the word.

Surrender

"When you are completely caught up in something, you become oblivious to things around you, or to the passage of time. It is this absorption in what you are doing that frees your unconscious and releases your creative imagination."

Rollo May, *The Courage to Create*

Fear is living in the past.
Worry is living in the future.
To be happy, live in the present.

Surrender to what you're doing when you are doing it.

I have found that when I let go of a problem that I have been struggling with and focus all my attention on the work itself, the answer comes to me on its own. As I release myself from needing to control the outcome and surrender the result to a higher power, miracles happen. This sometimes occurs when I'm trying to write an article but can't even begin. As I let go of having to know exactly what the final form will be and concentrate on the writing itself—the ideas and the facts—it starts to take shape on its own.

I began my first consulting business after struggling for months to find a way I could work for myself with the skills I had and no extra capital. After wearing myself out from worrying and trying to find the answer, I let go and just focused on the work I was doing at the time, which was head-hunting. One day I happened to be speaking with a recruiter who was in the human resources department of a client company. As we were chatting, I asked her how long she had been working for the company. She said she was a consultant there on contract. I asked her what she had done before. She said she had worked in an employment agency (which was what *I* was doing) before she started her business. There was my answer! I had my first contract within three months.

Surrender doesn't mean giving up. It means giving in to your total attention and being. It means letting go of the outcome, expectations, and ego gratification. Surrender means committing entirely to what you are doing when you are doing it and allowing the answers to show themselves.

Try These:

1. If you are struggling, stop. Make a "Surrender Box." You can use any type of box you like. Write your worries on a card and put the card in the box. Then continue your work as if your problems are being taken care of. Surrender, let go of the outcome, and concentrate on the moment.
2. Place Post-It notes around the house to remind you to:

    Breathe   Slow Down   Observe   Listen

3. Notice synchronicity, better known as coincidence. For example, you are in a book shop and you open a book and find the answer to a question you've been struggling with. Or you're looking for a new job and someone you haven't seen in years calls you about a job or knows someone you should talk to about one.

"Do less, be more. Achieve less, have more."
Lao Tzu

4

Begin Your Future Now

~∞∞∞~

"If one advances confidently in the
direction of his own dreams, and
endeavors to live the life which he has
imagined, he will meet with a success
unexpected in common hours."

Henry David Thoreau

"What you are is what you have been,
what you will be is what you do now."

Buddha

*The Universe gives us what we need when
we need it.*

*You have to reinvent yourself every once in
a while.*

Remember the Feelings of "YES!"

The first step in realizing a life dream is in identifying, seeing, and feeling it.

Do you remember the feeling of "YES!"—the excitement you felt about the first day of school, of when you first fell in love, or of when you were so engrossed in what you were doing that time flew and you forgot to look at the clock? Did you have those feelings when you were discovering a new place, a new friend, or a solution to a problem? Or was it the smell of books or soil or tools or paints that aroused such feelings? Or the feel of fabrics or clay? Or the thrill of building something?

Try These:

1. List times in your life when you had feelings of "YES!" What were you doing? Give a few examples.
2. Where have you had similar feelings recently—at work or at home, with friends or all alone? Were you by yourself, building a team, getting a product out, selling, mentoring, reading a good book, playing a sport or game?
3. Name one thing you could do this week that would give you similar feelings of "YES!" Write it down and do it by this time next week. Next week, choose something else.

Example:

When I was a kid I loved to ride a bicycle. I loved the freedom I felt as the wind rushed through my hair. I loved riding off by myself away from home and discovering new places in my town. Today, I have those same feelings when I discover a new place or book that I love. I also get those feelings when I start a new project or a new business. I love the exhilaration of discovering and beginning.

Create Your Personal Vision

"If you don't know where you're going, any road will
take you there."

Anonymous

*A vision acts as a beacon. It guides you back to where you
want to go.*

When I left my corporate job to start my own business, I knew
I had been given another chance. This was a new beginning. I
was in my late forties and wanted the next half of my life to fit
in with who I really was and how I wanted to live. This was
now the time.

There was much I had loved about my previous jobs. There
were also a lot of things that I didn't want to repeat. I had loved
the traveling—Europe, Asia, all of North America—but I knew
I didn't want to spend the rest of my life on a plane. Some of
my most exciting work had come from working with teams
under stressful deadlines. Although I loved the dynamic energy,
I hated the stress and didn't want that lifestyle. My body
agreed.

However, I was going into uncharted territory and was nervous. Although I knew what I didn't want, I wasn't clear about
what I did want. I took some time and did a visualization exercise to start the process of creating my vision for my future. I
saw myself living in the country, surrounded by books, writing,
coaching, leading seminars, connecting with creative people,
and having the time I wanted to draw, travel, and spend with
my family. I was then able to start taking ministeps to start
doing *now* some of what I saw myself doing in the future. I
opened a coaching practice with an office in my home in the
suburbs of Boston and led outplacement workshops for companies that were downsizing. I also created Doing Work You
Love seminars at Interface, a holistic adult education institute

in Cambridge. I then started writing articles, a newsletter, and this book as well as coaching via telephone and the Internet. I enrolled in an art class and made my dining room into a quasi-studio. I was setting the foundation for my future while doing what I loved doing *today*. That's what I want for you!

Whom do you want to talk to all day? Or do you want to talk to anyone at all?

Try These:

1. Sit quietly and close your eyes. Using the items listed below, picture vividly in your imagination how you would like your future to be. Add to that picture how you would like to be feeling in that future scene. Describe this experience in the present tense, as if it is already happening. Don't analyze what you want. Judging how reasonable or possible it is or how you could earn a living at it will get in the way of your creativity.
   - *How you are, how you look. (Example:* I am feeling healthy and have lots of energy. I am energetic, trim, good-looking, confident, charismatic, quiet, strong, peaceful, gentle, compassionate, powerful, etc.)
   - *Things you have.* Car, clothes, furnishings, boats, books, cameras, toys, etc. (*Example:* I feel great/proud/sexy/happy/excited/creative/confident/free having/owning/using my _____.
   - *People in your life.* What kinds of characteristics do they have (smart, honest, upbeat, easygoing, sophisticated, intellectual, laid back, casual, formal, etc.) and interests (similar to mine, different than mine, etc.)? How are you feeling with them (safe, supported, empowered, valued, etc.)?
   - *Where you are living.* Country, city, mountains, suburbs, near the ocean, U.S., Hong Kong. Type of house, fur-

nishings, decorations, gardens, etc. When you look out your living room window, what do you see? How do you feel?

- *Type of work you are doing, skills you are using.* How are you feeling as you do what you do? Close your eyes and imagine.

- *Do you picture yourself working with your hands or your body?* With books, people, ideas, art, crafts, or music? Are you inside or outside? How many hours a day/week/month are you working?

- *What kinds of products or services do you see yourself working with?* To answer this question ask yourself what you are learning. What are you talking about all day? Every industry has its own vocabulary. What language are you speaking? For example, do you want to be talking and learning about investments, art, technology, language, books, law, politics, health, medicine, fishing, skiing, golf, or what?

- *What level of responsibility do you have, and why?* Is it for status, for power, to be able to influence, to be in charge, to work by yourself, to work with a partner/team, to mentor, to be an authority, to make a difference, to live with less stress, or to make a lot of money? (There are no right or wrong answers.)

- *What are the day-to-day rhythms?* Are they calm, fast-paced, or a mixture? How many people are you interacting with every day? Do you see yourself in the center of a busy hub (e.g., airport, hotel, etc.), in a cabin in the woods, or somewhere in between?

- *What hobbies and other interests do you see yourself pursuing* (travel, crafts, sports, theater, reading, writing a novel, etc.)? If travel, make a list of where, including cities. If crafts or artistic/musical pursuits, be specific. Which ones?

- *What kinds of contributions do you want to make?* What do you want to leave behind?

2. Go over each part of the previous exercise. Where and how are you being, doing, or having any of those qualities or characteristics now? What ministeps could you start taking today to live your vision?

3. *What is getting in the way?* Some of what keeps you from having what you want is just day-to-day stuff you aren't handling. *Not* doing what continually whispers to you to take care of keeps you from having what you really want. What you resist, persists.

   • *Look at your personal environment.* What is gnawing at you that you should take care of (e.g., closets, taxes, wrinkled clothes, a malfunctioning car, the stuff on the cellar stairs, etc.)? Choose one and commit to complete it in one week.

   • *Look at your well-being.* What part of your emotional/physical/spiritual well-being needs more attention (e.g., a weekly exercise program, healthy diet, dentist/doctor visits, discontinuing toxic relationships, etc.)? Choose one thing and commit to address it within one week. Next week choose another. Notice the new energy you have when you complete just one task!

State *How* You Want to Be, Not *What* You Want to Be

You spend two-thirds of your waking hours in work-related activities. How do you want to feel during that time? What do you want to be moving toward? The future is now.

Nina was very unhappy with her job and didn't know what to do. Her work was a continual struggle. She was a systems analyst for a large medical insurer. She had been with her company for 12 years. She had fallen into her job after graduating college and had progressed over the years with increased responsibility and promotions. Although she was good at her work, she had never loved it. Nina wished she were a secretary. "Why?" I asked. "Because a secretary gets things done, is important, finishes projects, and can leave," was Nina's reply. Nina's work as a systems analyst had no end point and few boundaries. It was amorphous and gave her little satisfaction. As Nina started to define what was important to her, she saw that she wanted a job where she was in charge and could see an end result within a reasonable amount of time. She also knew she didn't want to supervise people. She was then able to incorporate her *desires* (structured projects with a defined ending where she could be in charge of results but not people) with her *skills* (analytical, detail oriented, thorough) and her *experience* (acquired business and systems understanding) into a new job as a project leader in her company. She would then be able to have the sense of accomplishment she had perceived a secretary as having. She talked to her manager about her goals, started networking within her company, and even negotiated a promotion for herself to do the work she wanted.

Try These:

1. What do you fantasize about being—either in a career or in your personal life? What are the qualities that appeal to you? In what other areas of your life could you experience those feelings?

   Example:

   Do you want to be a pilot? What about being a pilot appeals to you? Being above ground? Flying? The freedom, sense of control, being in charge, by yourself, etc.

2. Time yourself for 60 seconds and list 10 things that you enjoy most in life. How do they make you feel? Where else could you experience those feelings? How could you incorporate any of these into your life on a daily or weekly basis? How might you have these feelings in the work you do?

Choosing Doesn't Have to Be Forever

"One cannot collect all the beautiful shells on the beach."
Anne Morrow Lindbergh

We are very lucky. We live in one of the richest, most opportunity-laden countries in the world. There are uncountable careers to choose from, places to live, things to buy, people to know. The number of choices is often so mind-boggling that it paralyzes us. If we choose one, we might miss out on another. And what if we make a mistake? So we don't choose or commit for fear of missing out on *all* the other opportunities that we *aren't* choosing. You've probably known people who avoid committing to a relationship because they're waiting for Prince or Princess Charming. Some people also spend their lives waiting for Job Charming, hoping it might be just around the corner if they only wait long enough!

There is no Job Charming, and choosing doesn't have to be forever. There are no Choosing Police, either.

Annie had originally loved teaching at the local university but had become increasingly dissatisfied with her job. For her, far more satisfaction came from her volunteer work or from entertaining her many friends. Annie was approaching 40 and wanted more joy in her work life as she became older. She didn't want to continue working in academia and was searching for something that she could be more passionate about. I asked her what she really enjoyed doing, what was fun, and what her friends acknowledged her for. She blushed and said, "It's really quite silly."

I thought, "That's it!" What we do for fun and are sometimes embarrassed to admit to anyone often holds a key to our passion. "What is it?" I asked gently.

"I like to wrap presents," she said. When I asked her to explain, I learned that for Annie wrapping gifts was an art, albeit one she sheepishly acknowledged. During the year Annie collected various materials to have on hand when she needed them for special occasions. These materials might consist of ribbons from the florist, various fabrics and papers she would find on her travels, or pieces of shells or twigs or acorns. Sometimes she would paint a mural on a large piece of brown paper and use that to wrap an object. Her friends and family often framed these paintings. Although Annie was not interested in a gift-wrapping business, she wanted to be open to other possibilities where she could use her artistic talents.

Annie also shyly admitted that she was known in her town for her dinners. I asked what she meant. She said she was a gourmet cook who created meals around a theme so that she could also decorate the dining room to reflect the theme. With some more prodding, Annie talked excitedly about her house and how she had designed the kitchen and some of the furnishings. She had also landscaped the yard. As I listened and coached her, she began to envision other careers that she might like. She ultimately decided upon three that might fit into her lifestyle. It was important to Annie that she have time to spend with her husband at night and on weekends. She chose to explore what would be involved in becoming a landscape architect, kitchen designer, or interior designer.

I asked Annie to select one possibility at a time and to commit to learning as much as she could about it within a two-week period. If she needed more time, we would extend it another two weeks. However, once she had chosen she had to commit 500 percent to that choice for the entire two weeks. Her homework was to try out being a landscape architect for that period of time. She was to read articles about landscape design, connect with associations of landscape designers, and review course catalogs of landscape-design schools. She was to learn what professionals did, how they found clients, how much they earned, etc. I requested that she notice how she felt as she talked to at least three people who were in that business and asked them some of the questions in exercise #2 on page 88.

Could she see herself in this role? Since Annie and I had already discussed what qualities were important to her in her life, she was also interviewing these people to learn how their careers might fit into her time, financial, and life requirements.

Annie did her homework. At each session she reported her findings, what she liked and didn't like about that period's career. She examined the return on the investment she would be making in terms of both time and money, as she knew she would need to go back to school. She also learned that she was excited about some of the courses at an interior-design school in Boston and enrolled in one class while she continued to teach at the university. Annie was so successful in her first class that her teacher asked her to help him work with a design client— something unheard-of for a part-time, first-year student! That experience showed Annie that interior design was what she wanted to do. Annie still calls me periodically to report on her progress and to tell me how happy she is. She is still doing some teaching as she completes her schooling and is even beginning to get some clients of her own.

Try This:

1. Make a list of the things you would like to do. Then choose one. Commit to it for one month (or whatever period of time seems appropriate). Talk to people who are already doing what you want to be doing. Commit 500 percent to learning as much as you can about your chosen pursuit. Once you have chosen what it is and for how long, you must stay committed to that choice for the entire time period. Then at the end of that period, reassess. Either recommit fully for another period of time or remove the pursuit from your list of desires. Just choose! Carrying the fantasy is getting in your way. It is extra mind-baggage.

   This exercise can work in your current job too. For example, if you can't decide whether to stay or leave your current place of employment, choose a time period to commit 500 percent to doing the best job possible. Go all out! At the end of that time period, reassess your job. Then either recommit 500 percent or put your energy into looking somewhere else. Work in increments—not the rest of your life! Things change and so do you!

2. If you are trying on different careers or jobs, choose one for one to three months. During that time, talk to at least three people who do what you are thinking of doing. Ask them questions from the following list that are important to you:

- How did you get into this work?
- What do you like/dislike most about it?
- What do you do in a typical day?
- What type of people do you work with? What are they like?
- Whom do you sell to? Who are your clients/customers? Whom do you buy from? (You might discover you want that job or create one that doesn't exist yet. Ask for referrals.)
- What is your organization (or project) trying to accomplish?
- To what level of management do you report? Could you describe the management structure here?
- How much autonomy do you have?
- What is the salary range for this type of work/position? (You're not asking them how much *they* make, but what you can expect for this type of career. Yes, this is a legitimate question.)
- What kind of support does management provide? Do you need training, seminars, travel, support staff, office space, equipment, mentoring, etc.?
- What is the morale like here?
- Is this industry/your company growing? Why or why not?
- What, in your opinion, is the job outlook in this career area/business?

- Whom else should I speak with about working in this industry/company?

  If, after speaking with at least three people, doing library research, connecting with associations, etc., you find you are no longer interested in a given career, cross it off your list and choose another. (But, please, don't enroll in and pay thousands of dollars for a training program right away. Don't commit to a new career without doing this work first!)

3. If, however, you are still interested, then start being that career. (Read Act As If You Are Already There on page 90.)
4. Design a picture for how this year will unfold for you. Hang it up on your wall.

Make your dreams your goals. Begin working now toward what you want to be doing in the future. For example, if your dream is to live in the country (and earn a living), you might begin by spending one weekend (or day) per month in different country settings. You might then choose to extend this period to see if you could live in a particular community and if the lifestyle is as satisfying as you had imagined. If it is, you might then start thinking in terms of how you could work there. What skills and interests could you expand? Could you telecommute to your current job for part of the month? How could you propose this to your management so they could see it as an advantage for them?

Try This:

1. On a clean sheet of paper, list 10 dreams you have and then brainstorm on paper how you could start doing them now. If you fill up the sheet, start on another.
2. Collect brochures, photos, advertisements, and descriptions of what your life will look like and put them on your walls where you can see them. Or create a collage out of the collected items.

Act As If You Are Already There

A myth many of us still believe is that we need some other person or institution to give us permission (a certificate, formal training, or a blessing) before we can be or do what we want. This is true only if you need a license for it!

I Am a Coach and Seminar Leader

When I decided that I wanted to be a seminar leader and coach, I sent out flyers offering workshops in my home. I told my friends, and people came. Some who came referred their friends, clients, or colleagues to me for career coaching and other seminars. At the same time I was also looking for assignments to deliver outplacement seminars in companies that were laying off employees. When people asked me what I did, I said "I am a coach and seminar leader," and then they hired me to do coaching and run seminars. I wasn't officially trained or certified to do this, and no one gave me permission. I didn't know I needed it. So when clients ask me what training they need to do something, I usually say, "Just do it!"

Declare what it is you want to be and then *be* it. For example, if you want to be a writer, tell yourself, "I am a writer." Then *write*. Then take classes (if you choose) to increase your craft because you *are* a writer. You will be more powerful and confident because you actually see yourself as a writer. You may not yet be supporting yourself as a writer, but you will be creating your future in the present every day.

If you want to do something but a company won't let you because you don't have the credentials, find another company or get the credentials.

Try These:

1. Pretend it is five years from now and an article has just been written about you in your favorite magazine. In which magazine will it appear? Now write the article.

2. Declare and live from your goal. For example, if you want to be an entrepreneur, tell yourself, "I am an entrepreneur." Then ask yourself how you can be an entrepreneur in your daily activities (e.g., by what you read, what you do, the ideas you have, how you approach your work, your future plans, etc.). Then act as if you are an entrepreneur in your present job. What improvements could you make? How would you increase sales? Also, do research that will support your goal for having your own business in the future. You are now not only acting out being an entrepreneur, you are living your dream daily.

If a Writer Isn't Writing, Is He Still a Writer?

My friend Robert writes and produces scientific documentaries. Many of his films have appeared on public television networks both here and in Great Britain. Robert has worked for others, has had his own company, and has won numerous awards for his work. He is fascinated by science and is constantly investigating projects he finds interesting. He speaks with leading scientists and scholars around the world, develops and writes about new ideas, and constantly sends out proposals. However, he is not always *paid* for his efforts and he has periods when he does no writing at all. Nevertheless, Robert considers himself a writer and producer of scientific documentaries whether or not he is writing and whether or not someone buys his ideas.

Try asking yourself these questions:

1. If his film idea is not being funded at the moment, or if he is in a dry period or having writer's block, is Robert still a writer and producer? Who says so?
2. If you are an actor or dancer or sculptor or _____, and are supporting yourself financially by doing something else, you are still an actor or dancer or sculptor or _____. How are you being that in your daily activ-

ities (e.g., classes you take, auditions, people you hang out with, clothes you wear, the way you describe yourself, etc.)?

Who says so? *You* say so. And that's *all* you need.

Don't Ask Permission!

It only gives someone else more work.

Frequently clients and people who attend my seminars ask me if it's all right to call someone whom they do or don't know with the intention of asking for help. Or they may ask if it's OK to market their services or to develop a new project where they are. As most of these people are new to self-employment, they are unaware of *Self-Employment Rule #1*:

It's better to apologize later than to wait for permission.

I learned this rule many times over the years and it was in direct contrast with what I had previously believed. So I am never surprised when others (of every age) ask me, "Is it all right to . . . ?" Self-Employment Rule #1 holds true whether you are working for someone else or for yourself. Asking permission not only gives someone else more work, it also undermines your commitment to accomplishing your goal. Besides, if you're like I was, you're impatient, you have bills to pay, and you're determined to succeed. I learned that if I waited for someone to give me permission, I delayed achieving the results I wanted. Of course, I would have had someone to blame for not being able to succeed; that person or group that I thought I needed permission from. Although that may have felt good, I still would not have accomplished my goal. I would also have been asking others to take the time to make a decision for which *they* would be responsible. Since busy people don't have much time, it is easier for them to just say no. I learned to just do it and accept responsibility for the outcome. This *usually* worked to my benefit.

One key question I coach clients to ask prospective employers is: "How do you reward people who have taken a risk and failed?" If the answer is, "They don't fail," then it's easy to see that this company is *not* an innovator. Innovation requires risk and independent-minded people with self-employed attitudes.

Asking permission is giving up your power and not accepting responsibility for the outcome.

There are organizations where it may *seem* as though you are not allowed to do anything without a boss's permission. It may also *appear* as though there are unwritten rules that say you have to do things in a particular way. But look more closely. Find out if your impression is really true or if it is your belief system at work.

We act as if beliefs and appearances are the whole truth.

Janis is a talker. She is also attractive, vivacious, and fun. She loves to be with people, gab, help, and get to know them. Janis used to hate her job. For two years she toyed with leaving it and doing something else. She loved to draw, but she didn't want to earn her living as an artist. When she came to my seminar, she had been doing systems management work for a large health care provider. She spent her days glued to the phone and computer answering employees' questions about the software they were using. She knew she was helping people but wondered why she was feeling so depressed. Janis's energy was being boxed inside her cubicle. She was an active person, and she realized she needed interaction where she could both be with others *and* move around. She also saw that since the company was changing over to personal computers, she could train everyone—in person. She started offering her help and soon became known as the PC resource. Janis didn't ask for permission. She just did it. Her management gave her support once they saw how effective she was. She then set up a customer service hot line, trained others to do what she was doing, and later received from her employer an Outstanding Performer Award for her innovation. No one gave her permission to help her clients in a way that most served both their needs and hers!

Try Answering This:

Think about your current job, dream career, and relationships. Ask yourself what you would like to do that you think you need permission to do. Do you *really* need permission? What would happen if you just did it and were successful?

> Until one is committed there is hesitancy, the chance to draw back, always ineffectiveness. Concerning all acts of initiative and creation, there is one elementary truth, the ignorance of which kills countless ideas and splendid plans: that the moment one definitely commits oneself, then providence moves too. All sorts of things occur to help one that would otherwise never have occurred. A whole stream of events issues from the decision, raising in one's favor all manner of unforeseen incidents and meetings and material assistance, which no man could have dreamt would have come his way.
>
> Johann Wolfgang Goethe

5

Uncover Your Purpose

∞

"Our deepest fear is not that we are
inadequate; our deepest fear is that we
are powerful beyond all measure."

Marianne Williamson

*Your purpose is to let your spirit—your
essence—shine forth. Your purpose will
support your vision no matter what you are
doing. Your spirit speaks through what calls
to you, what you love to do, and where you
want to do it. Your purpose is to share your
essence with others.*

Keep It Simple

"When you are able to shift your central focus to how
you serve others, you will be in a position to know
true miracles in your progress towards prosperity."
John Donovan

We are a spiritual people. Many of us follow a religious tradition; others define spirituality for themselves. We yearn for soul in our work; we long to make a difference. In a culture that deifies pop singers, movie stars, and CEOs, where companies lay off thousands when profits are increasing, it is hard not to ask, "What is wrong with this picture? What is my life really about? Why am I here? What am I supposed to be doing?" Men and women have been seeking the answers to these questions since time began.

Clients frequently tell me they want work that is meaningful; they seek a purpose for their lives. They feel there is something missing and that their work should be more than just a means to earn a living. Most fell into their first job and developed a career from there. Others pursued paths that their parents or teachers had dictated for them. And years later they realize there is a void in their lives.

Although Mark was a senior manager for a real estate company, he was dissatisfied with the progress he was making in his career. He felt there was something fundamental missing, but he couldn't put his finger on it. He had been lucky with sales. He liked building relationships with his clients, doing deals, and supporting his staff. He wanted to do more but felt hampered by the company politics and his own feelings of inadequacy. (Those feelings!) We reviewed his history and interests. Mark had a lot of friends, many whom he had known since boyhood. Supporting his friends and family was important to him and he kept in touch with those who had moved away. Some of Mark's passions were American history, historical renovation, and his city's history. After some reflection, he saw the ties between the work he did in real estate, the relationships he built, and his interest in history and community. He carved out a life purpose that was larger than the day-to-day annoyances that were getting in his way. Once he realized that his purpose was "to help build communities where people live well," he started approaching his work differently. Little problems disappeared. His purpose became the umbrella for his future vision. He was then able to see that his goal to be president of a company—either someone else's or his own—was in line with his overall purpose and that his daily work supported this vision. He saw the impact that a leadership role could have on the communities where he lived and that all the pieces of his life had been and were in support of this goal. His communities were within his job, family, town, church, social life, sports activities, and interests. They were where he played out his different roles of manager, husband, friend, nurturer, mentor, organizer, parent, son, home owner, etc. He could *live* his purpose every day, and was he psyched!

> *It is in our ordinary lives that we create miracles, unknowingly.*

I was explaining to my friend Jim this struggle to find purpose. Jim teaches economics at a local university. Although his heart was in teaching, Jim was feeling increasing pressure to publish more in order to stay competitive. He reflected on his own situation and said that he felt very fortunate that his field was environmental economics, which was currently important, although it had been less so when he had started his career 30 years earlier. However, he added, he knew his real purpose was teaching and mentoring and that the subject of economics was his vehicle to do both these things. This was an "aha" for him. It was something he hadn't articulated before.

Is what you do the vehicle that allows your spirit to shine forth? Most people have more than one purpose. For example, in a person's role as parent, spouse, or friend, one purpose might be to nurture and support his or her children, partner, or friends. Perhaps this purpose carries over into their work or maybe there are other purposes to define.

Try these exercises to help you define your purpose(s). Write your answers on a clean sheet of paper.

1. What service do you provide?
2. Fill in this blank: I _____

Examples:

I help people have fun.
I help people be healthy.
I help people be happy.
I help people have the quality of life that they want.
I provide joy wherever I go.
I provide a safe, nurturing home for my family.
I provide humor (beauty, services, information, etc.)
I am a loving, caring person.
I enjoy life.

3. Fill in the blanks: And I do this by_____
   (singing, listening, teaching, serving, being funny, nurturing, etc.)
   I also do this by_____.

Example:

My purpose is to help people honor themselves. I do this by supporting who they are, offering encouragement, and providing a safe place for them to be. I also do this by coaching, writing, and leading seminars.

How are you already fulfilling your purpose? Your purpose is reflected in what you do in your life, the values you live by, and who you are. The problem is in your limited viewpoint. You are standing too close to your various roles. Make them bigger. What do you bring forth into the world? What do you do in your day-to-day work, your weekly activities? How is your current work a stepping-stone to another goal that supports your purpose?

Part of what stops us from gaining satisfaction is that we think what we do should be different, important, or significant. It already is.

Look at Your Themes

The only thing I knew for certain when I left corporate life was that I needed a rest. I wanted three months to relax, quiet down, and reenergize my body, mind, and soul. I wanted to use this time to clean out the closets of my life and begin anew. I spent the three months reconnecting with my kids, my friends, and my self. As I then reflected on my past, I was able to see some common themes in my eclectic careers:

1. I had always been driven to find jobs where I could use my skills, learn more, and earn more money.
2. Work and my kids were my overarching focus.
3. I outgrew jobs every two years and needed to be continually learning and growing.
4. I had had a lot of job changes and work experiences.
5. I had always been interested in personal development.

I also realized that I wanted to use these experiences to benefit others while at the same time do work I loved and be able to grow and expand. That is still what I am doing and what I want for my clients and for you.

Betsy had always been the responsible one in her family, whether she liked it or not. Although Betsy lived and worked as a school administrator in another state, and although her brother and sister lived nearer their elderly mother, Betsy was the one charged with caring for her. Betsy arranged her mother's medical care, reconciled her checking accounts, payed her bills, and resolved her billing problems. After five years of giving long-distance care, she moved her mother to a nursing home closer to where she lived. Betsy had researched housing, arranged movers, and orchestrated the sale of her mother's property—all while working full time. After her mother's death three years later, Betsy realized how dissatisfied she had become with her job, its politics, and the cutbacks. She had been in education for almost 20 years and thought that was all she knew. After some soul-searching, Betsy decided to start a business offering the same service she had long provided for her family—as a personal ombudsman for the elderly. She researched the competition and interviewed nursing homes, social workers, and available services. She had been careful and had enough savings to support her business for a few years while it was getting off the ground. She developed a marketing plan, a targeted mailing list from hundreds of contacts, an attractive brochure, and business cards. Betsy resigned from her school job and went to work. She now has a successful business where she is doing what she has always done well—taking care of others, organizing, and making sure people's needs are met.

All of your previous experience has brought you to where you are today. These are your tools and your training. You are like the artist who has spent years studying academic painting in order to create her own style. This style is continually evolving and refining itself.

> "So long as you continually have the desire to learn
> more and understand more and want to keep
> discovering things, then you're always fresh."
> Ken Done

This is a clarifying exercise to help you along your path to defining your purpose. Try asking yourself these questions:

1. What are your landmark events?
2. What has given you the most satisfaction in your life?
3. What have you continually struggled with (work, relationships, money, alcohol, weight, creativity, etc.)?
4. What drives you? How could what drives you benefit others?
5. What's the common theme of your passions?
6. Who are your role models and mentors? What are their qualities that you most admire? When do you mirror those qualities?
7. If money were no problem, what would you do?
8. How can you use your gifts, talents, experiences, and struggles to be of service?

Listen to Your Longings

"My life is my message."

Mahatma Gandhi

"Integrity is having the courage and self-discipline to live by your inner truth."

Jack Hawley

When Andy came to see me, she had been a therapist for more than 16 years and was feeling burned out. The mental health care field had changed a lot since the time when she had chosen it as a career. And she had changed a lot too. Andy was forced to see too many patients and wasn't allowed to spend much time with any one of them. She had doubts about how much she was helping her patients. She wanted a change but didn't know where to start.

When Andy spoke about her life, what she had done from childhood to the present, what interested her and what she liked doing that was "silly," I watched her face and listened to her language. She lit up when she spoke about the Southwest,

Indian rugs, the warm colors of New Mexico, and her love of animals. Andy had worked in Africa and Guatemala as an animal behaviorist before she became a psychotherapist; however, she had ruled out working in a zoo or pursuing further training to become a veterinarian. Her hobbies included beadwork and making crafts for friends. She spoke excitedly of muted and vibrant colors, of the land, of sun and warmth, of textures and tones. She had fallen in love with the Zapotec rugs she and her husband had seen on a trip to Santa Fe five years earlier. She decided to call the owners of the shop where they had purchased their rug to see how she could sell such rugs in New England. The shop owners told her she needed $10,000 to start. She had only $5,000. At my suggestion, Andy attended the Small Business Association (SBA) entrepreneur program to gather information on starting her own business. She gained valuable tips and met new contacts. Her husband, Marty, an engineer, had initially been skeptical about this plan. However, the more he listened to her excitement, her love of the rugs, and the research she had done, the more enthusiastic he became. He too began to study the craft involved and the differences in dyes, designs, qualities, and weavers. In other words, he became Andy's business partner. They visited the Santa Fe shop owners together and were eventually able to negotiate purchasing $5,000 worth of rugs and the other $5,000 on consignment. It was also important to Andy that the rugs were not being produced in sweatshops. She did more research and visited the artists who made them. Happily reassured, Andy and Marty changed their living room into a showroom and invited decorators, shop owners, and friends to their opening. Southwest Weavers was born.

Try These:

1. Look at the common threads that bind together all your interests and longings. What insights can you gain?
2. What makes you truly happy?

What Makes You Fearful, Angry, Impatient?

Sometimes the biggest battles in our lives are the ones that motivate us the most.

Carolyn had grown up in a middle-class family of very modest means. She had been raised to believe that someday her prince would come and she'd live happily ever after. He didn't show up, however, and she needed to earn a living. Her parents had also told her she shouldn't worry about her future, that she should go to school and then marry. After college, with no wedding on the horizon, she was in a panic. She was terrified of being poor, and angry that she had been lied to by her well-meaning parents. She decided she would not only earn a sizable income but would also make sure other women had more information about money than she had had. She would have her own business. Carolyn spent the next 10 years with a large insurance company and took courses in financial management. It took her seven years to become certified and another three to establish her business. Today Carolyn is a highly respected financial planner. When she isn't meeting with clients or networking, she is giving seminars on money management at local adult education centers and colleges. Her fear and anger paid off not only by motivating her to ensure her own financial security but also by giving her life meaning as she teaches others how to take care of themselves too.

Try These:

1. What makes you angry?
2. What are you most afraid of?
3. What has been a consistent struggle for you throughout your life? How would you like to make it different for someone else?

Love and Integrity at Work

Vitality comes through integrity. Integrity means right action, right thinking, and being true to yourself.

Love is relevant at work. What is love? Love is patience, respect, honor, care, action, partnership, compassion, helping, welcoming, commitment, and keeping your word.

I've held positions where all I cared about were results. I was so deadline-driven that I forgot the things that were most important to me. These were the same things my clients were later to tell me were missing from *their* lives: soul, time for friends, relationships that count, beauty, music, caring, nurturing, compassion, and spirit.

When my clients explore how to bring those qualities to their work lives, they say, "Pay attention, listen more, slow down, look people in the eye, honor yourself, practice patience and respect, show up on time, keep your word, listen to your intuition, and bring beauty to work."

Try These:

1. What's missing in your life?
2. How can you bring what's missing into your work and personal life every day?

Honor your answers and try making them part of your life daily.

6

Look for Options

❦

You will experiment and tumble. Try things on until you find the right fit.

Option 1: Where You Are

Start with today.

You may not have to leave your present job or company in order to do what you love. Remember Nina, who found a job as a project leader, and Janis, who created a new career as a trainer, in the companies they were already working for. You may be able to do it too.

Jim, a sales engineer, came to the Doing Work You Love seminar because he was dissatisfied with his job. In the workshop, he was able to see he was repeating the same patterns with his present company that he had done with others: the first four months were great, and then he lost interest, found fault with his bosses and the company, and started looking for another job. He saw he had been waiting for them to give him permission to start new projects and tell him he was OK. Jim discovered that he really *liked* what he was doing. He realized that if he wanted to do something he could just plan it and do it. When he returned to his company, he started taking charge of things he felt needed to be changed. He also began to initiate projects he had thought of doing. He said he "stopped waiting and just did it." What surprised him most was the new level of respect he was getting from his bosses and everyone around him.

Jim's story reminds me of the one about the man in Africa who won a huge oil field in a poker game. He was excited by his prize and worked day and night looking for his wealth. Although he drilled for years he was only able to locate a few minor wells. The man finally gave up in disgust and sold the land. With his earnings, he moved his family to New York City, bought a taxicab, and started a new life.

The new owner of the oil field chose a different approach. He decided not to drill for oil, but to explore the land to see what else he could find. He discovered numerous caves that

contained raw diamonds. He had purchased acres of diamonds—and all the riches that had eluded the first owner.

Try This:

Before you change jobs or companies, try to see if there are
diamonds where you are right now.

Option 2: Somewhere Else

When Paul decided to leave his job, he knew he wanted to stay
in publishing. He had spent his career there, liked the industry,
and had developed a large network of supportive friends and
colleagues. Eight years earlier, he had moved from production
to sales, a change that had given him the flexibility and income
he had wanted. Now Paul wanted to travel less, have fewer
worries, and spend more time with his wife and children. His
present company wasn't able to accommodate him, so Paul
decided to look somewhere else.

He had a number of offers and chose one as manager of
operations for a small company that provided typesetting services to publishing companies. He liked the president/owner
and the people who worked there. Although the company was
located farther from his home than he would have liked, his
management offered him the flexibility to telecommute from
his house a few days a week and arrange his hours for when the
traffic was lighter. Paul had found a job in the industry he
loved, doing work that fit how he wanted to live at this time in
his life. His wife and kids loved it too—they could have him
home more often.

Try These:

1. Ask yourself: Is it the job, the company, or the industry you
   are in that is causing your dissatisfaction?

2. Some industries may only allow for a certain lifestyle that is no longer compatible with how you want to live. If this is true in the field where you work, ask yourself where else you could take your experience from this industry. Who are your company's vendors or customers? Choose one and network to find out. Then choose another.

Option 3:
On Your Own or with Partners

The good news about having your own business is that you get to do work you love. The bad news is that you get to do it *all* the time. Perhaps you need a partner with different strengths.

When my kids had finished school and were exchanging their jeans for suits and backpacks for briefcases, they looked at me with troubled expressions and asked, "Have you ever had a job that you loved all the time?" They were having difficulty imagining working with only two weeks of vacation a year. They were also intimately aware of my varied career moves. I was now able to answer, "Yes, the one I'm doing today." Although I don't love the noncreative parts (e.g., paperwork, bills, marketing), neither do I hate them. I know they are part of my larger vision, so I just do them. Or I find someone else to do them.

My work is like a love affair, totally consuming. I am either writing, reading, designing seminars, marketing, or doing paperwork. I also have the time and flexibility to take a break during the day and walk, paint, or see friends and work on weekends if I want to. I find what I'm doing endlessly fascinating and I attract others who are also interested in creative ways of working and living. I have found my bliss, as Joseph Campbell would have said. Or my bliss has found me.

At various times I also take on partners whose strengths and ways of thinking are different from mine. We work on projects together, brainstorm ideas, and contribute to each others' work and creativity. It's fun too!

Try These:

1. Ask yourself if you would prefer to work alone or with a partner. Why? How could a partner help you?
2. If you prefer having a partner, what qualities would your perfect work partner have? What skills and style would complement yours? For example, if you know that your strengths are not in sales and marketing, find someone with those skills. Of if you hate balancing your checkbook and numbers are a mystery, look for a partner with a knack for accounting.
3. Who do you know who would be a good work partner? Propose your venture to them or network through them.

Option 4:
Do Whatever You Do with Distinction

"Each man has his own vocation. The talent is the call. He inclines to do something which is easy to him, and good when it is done, but which no other man can do. He has no rival. For the more truly he consults his own powers, the more difference will his work exhibit from the work of any other."

Ralph Waldo Emerson,
"Spiritual Laws"

The way you approach your work will distinguish you from all others.

Remember the story about the acres of diamonds (page 109)? Your acres of diamonds may be waiting within you.

Scott had a small contracting business doing odd jobs for home owners. His services included washing windows, changing storm doors, cleaning up after winter storms, and doing light yard work. He and the friends he hired prided themselves on the quality of their work and their attention to detail. They thought about what they or their parents would like if *they* were paying for such services. Not only did they clean up after they finished each job, but they would always remove their shoes before entering the customer's house so as not to track in debris. Scott always had plenty of customers; he financed his college education himself. Now in his twenties, he continues to distinguish himself, this time as the number one salesperson for a major corporation. He is still paying attention to the details.

Try This:

How could you do what you are currently doing with such a difference as to distinguish yourself from the competition? Who would your clients be?

Option 5:
Barter, Give It Away, and See What Happens

What you give away comes back to you a thousand times.

Gayle teaches people in the graphic arts and printing industries how to use Macintosh computers. She was originally an art teacher and became interested in computer graphics when her state eliminated art from public school curriculums. She took two classes at a local college that resulted in two jobs because of connections through her teacher. A go-getter, Gayle had her eye on one particular company that produced state-of-the-art

Macintosh software. She learned the company's product, attended the same trade shows, and networked for two years before they hired her. After another two years they laid her off in a reorganization. By this time Gayle had ideas she wanted to pursue on her own. She did some creative bartering with other companies and persuaded them to send her to some specialized training for advanced computer graphics; in exchange she would train their staff free of charge. Three months after being laid off, she had her first paying client. Her business has continued to grow. She is constantly sought after and does no marketing. Companies across the country hear about her by word of mouth. Gayle says her mission is to make people feel good about themselves while she is teaching them. She learned what she needed to use her teaching as a vehicle for her purpose.

Try This:

What could you give away or barter to move you closer to your dreams? For more ideas, read entrepreneurial magazines such as *Inc., Entrepreneur,* and *Success,* as well as local business newspapers, etc.

Option 6:
Teach What You Want to Learn

Just do it!

I used to teach yoga. I knew if I were teaching it, I would practice more and be forced to learn all I could. So I offered yoga classes at the local adult education program, opened a yoga studio, bought every book on yoga I could find, attended yoga classes three times a week, and became certified. In that order.

Try These:

1. Make a list of your passions and interests. Which would you like to learn more about? How could you teach it? What about volunteering?
2. If money were no problem, what would you like to study or learn? For how long? What would you like to learn after that?
3. How does what you want to learn fit into your vision for your future?

"To teach is to learn twice."

Joseph Joubert

Option 7: Organize Others

Perhaps one of your talents holds the keys to someone else's needs.

When Melissa became tired of the dating scene, she decided to start her own business. She hated bars, had taken every course at the adult education center, and didn't want to invest hundreds of dollars in a dating service. She thought there had to be a better way and created her own. She placed a small ad in a local magazine and Table for Eight was born. Melissa arranges dinners for eight people—four men and four women—who don't know each other. She prescreens them on the phone and matches them according to their ages and interests. Her dinners are held at choice restaurants. This innovative dating service has developed a following. Melissa has created a thriving business, has control of her time, and might even meet the man of her dreams.

Try This:

Which of your skills, gifts, and/or experiences might be useful to someone else? Think about what you do easily. How might that gift be helpful for someone who doesn't possess it?

When Rose thought about which of her skills she might use to start her own business, she knew that making order out of chaos was easy for her. (As I mentioned earlier, I am in awe of someone with such talents!) Rose decided to offer her services to people who needed help organizing their offices and homes or packing for a move. She called her business The Clutter Buster. I referred Rose to one of my friends whose office was filled with piles of magazines, articles, and books that hadn't been weeded through in years. Rose's intention was not only to help my friend organize her office but also to teach her how to do it on her own. She was successful with the discarding and arranging. However, as for training my friend to do it on her own, my friend's talents do not lie in organizing chaos, nor will they ever. Rose has a client for life.

Option 8: Choose an Alternative

As the Baby Boomer population ages, the desire for robust health and longevity has increased. No longer willing to rely totally on modern medicine, we have turned our attention to preventive treatments and natural remedies. We exercise more; limit dietary fats and preservatives; take vitamins, herbs, and homeopathic treatments. Chiropractic, acupuncture, and massage, which were once thought to be strictly New Age practices, have gone mainstream and are now covered by many health insurance policies. Many careers that were considered obscure 20 years ago are flourishing today as people sort out the best ways to live in a world of uncertainties.

My friend Lynn Robinson was an operations manager for a software company when she started moonlighting by giving psychic readings. She had first noticed her psychic gifts when she was a child and didn't make much of them. Then when she was in high school, she became interested in metaphysics and decided to let her intuition guide her to her life purpose. Over the next 12 years she did administrative work and returned to school for a master's degree. She also gave occasional readings for her friends, family, and certain coworkers. One day in 1987, she went to a friend's funeral and took the only available seat. The person sitting next to her was a reporter from one of the city's major newspapers. Coincidence? The reporter later interviewed Lynn and wrote a full-page article about her and her psychic readings. Lynn's business was born. She soon had so many clients that she was able to leave her operations job and do intuitive counseling full-time. She has a lovely office in Newton, MA, a two-month waiting list, and work that she loves—all the time.

Another friend, Deb Fournier, had climbed the ranks of human resources before she decided to become an acupuncturist. Deb was a senior staff member and didn't have a bachelor's degree. She had once started an undergraduate program, but had left for financial reasons and never completed it. The degree had not been necessary for her job. She was highly respected, earned a good salary, and had no desire to be a manager. However, one of the admissions requirements for acupuncture school was that she have a degree.

Deb enrolled in a university in Boston, 60 miles from her home, and entered a program that allowed her to go part-time and finish in three years. She also negotiated with her manager for four-fifths time so that she could have one day off a week for herself and her family. Over the next eight years, Deb received her Bachelor of Science degree and her acupuncture degree and license, took care of her family, and started her practice part-time. She opened her office doors in Leominster, MA, last summer to a waiting list of clients. Deb has created her dream—doing work that she loves, having a flexible schedule, and being able to help others—while earning a good living!

Try These:

1. What alternative careers have you thought of pursuing? Where could you find more information on them? Who could you talk to?
2. Any dream you choose to pursue will take time. How could you start taking ministeps toward your goal today?

Option 9: Watch the Trends

As I am always on the outlook for new ideas about careers and lifestyles, I was thrilled to find *Clicking* by Faith Popcorn and Lys Marigold. Faith Popcorn is the author of the bestseller *The Popcorn Report* and is also chairman of Brain Reserve, a marketing consulting firm that consults to Fortune 500 companies and helps them prepare for future business, lifestyle, and work trends. It was she who defined cocooning and cashing out before these words became part of our culture and vocabulary. In her most recent book, *Clicking*, she and Marigold uncover 16 trends that offer many opportunities for creating new products and services. Here are a few examples:

- *Cocooning.* The trend to stay safe and comfortable at home that she predicted years earlier in *The Popcorn Report* has been substantiated by the increased sales in burglar alarms, personal computers, home office equipment, direct-mail catalogs, and delivery services to name a few.
- *Fantasy Adventure.* Faith and Lys say that although we love the warmth and security of our homes, we still want some excite-

ment in our lives—but not *too* much. We buy computer action games, mountain bikes, and jeeplike vehicles (that *aren't* going on safari). We also purchase the products and services that make our lives more comfortable when we *do* go on safari, trek in the Himalayas, hike, rock climb, ski, scuba dive, or go hot-air ballooning.

• *Small Indulgences.* We give ourselves treats to offset our disappointments and anger that the myths we grew up with, such as job security and expected higher earnings, are not true. For example, notice the proliferation of expensive soaps and fragrances, exotic teas and juices, premium ice creams, herb-scented breads, costly pens, boutique hotels, spas, massage services, and supermarket flower stalls.

There are also the combined trends, such as linking fantasy adventure with small indulgences.

> Browse through a catalog such as J. Peterman Company's Owners Manual. Its owner started out with one product—a long canvas horseman's duster coat, advertised in places like *The New Yorker.* It clicked into consumers' imaginations by offering items with tales to tell. A hat modeled after Hemingway's, a tugboat captain's sweater, a David Niven blazer, a Gatsby shirt, a woman's long skirt like the one in *Out of Africa*, a blouse like Bacall's, Garbo pants. Last year the company pulled in $50 million dollars in sales.[9]

Another example of combining trends occurs when technology is joined with cocooning and egonomics. (Egonomics is the trend that appeals to our individuality and supports our insatiable desire for self-improvement. Note the success of self-help books, tapes, and videos.) For example, in *Newsweek* (February 5, 1996) Kendall Hamilton reported that "Tom Leonard, a former Salt Lake City financial planner, founded Coach University in 1992 to train potential coaches. This is a totally virtual institution. Would-be coaches can download expensive training 'modules' and self-administered tests from the Coach U Web page and dial into regularly scheduled conference-call 'TeleClasses.'" Coaches consult on everything from business, careers, relationships, spirituality, or a combination of all of these for fees ranging from $150 to $500 and up for four half-hour sessions a month. Since they coach by phone, they can do their work from the comfort of their home or boat and never get near morning traffic!

Try These:

To generate some new ideas:

1. Notice trends when you watch TV, shop, read magazines, or listen to the radio. Keep a journal about what you see.
2. Carry a small notebook in your pocket or bag. Whenever you have a new idea, write it down without judging it. Some of the most profitable businesses have come out of those ideas that just "happened" while their developers were doing something else.

Option 10:
Ten Different Ways to Do
What You Love

I thought I had read all the career and self-help books ever published and had vowed not to purchase one more. Then I spied Sarah and Paul Edwards's *Finding Your Perfect Work*. The Edwardses are gurus of consulting from home and starting your own business. They have written numerous books on these subjects. *Finding Your Perfect Work* offers many wonderful examples of people who have created unique careers with their talents and interests. I recommend it highly. This list comes from their book.

1. Do what you love.
2. Provide a service to others who do what you love.
3. Teach others to do what you love.
4. Write about what you love.
5. Speak about what you love.
6. Create a product related to what you love.
7. Sell or broker what you love.
8. Promote what you love.
9. Organize what you love.
10. Set up, repair, restore, fix, or maintain what you love.[10]

Stay Motivated

———∞∞∞———

"Eighty percent of success is just showing up."

Woody Allen

What to Do When the Blues Get You Down

"Anxiety is simply part of the condition of being human. If we were not anxious, we would never create anything."

William Barrett

It's loving what you do that will get you through the hard times.

Staying motivated when the going gets tough is not easy! It is the major challenge for everyone who decides to create a new life. Although we may create our own reality, overnight successes are extremely rare. We read about the end results—not the labors, frustrations, and black days. Those who succeed do so because they stay focused on their goals, deal with the setbacks, and hang in there long enough. They also pay attention to synchronicity, enlist support, take care of themselves, and create their own luck! They persist because they love what they are doing and can't think of any other way that they are willing to live.

Try These:

To help you through the blues:

1. *Be grumpy.* Or depressed or sad or disappointed. Give yourself a time limit. This can be an hour, a day, or a week. (No longer, please.) For this time period, really allow yourself to *be* disappointed, depressed, or sad. You don't have to make nice or pretend everything's OK or humor others. Give yourself permission to be as completely miserable as you want. However, at the end of that time period, stop. (You may want to forewarn your family and friends that you are

going to be grumpy for the period of time you choose so they can support you too.)

2. *Exercise.* This is *not* optional, this is very important. Physical exercise provides you with the vitality and mood balancing that your mind can't achieve alone. Physical movement increases endorphins and diminishes emotional upsets and depression. It is critical that you exercise at least 30 minutes a day. Start with 15 minutes and work up to 45. Something aerobic is best. Walking is fine, too.

3. *Talk to someone who isn't your mate.* Share what is going on in your life with a friend or counselor. Your mate already knows, wants to support you, and needs some relief. By talking with someone outside the relationship you will be supporting both of you.

4. *Keep a kudos folder.* Fill it with compliments, thank-you notes, old job reviews. It's a great reminder for those down days. Browse through it often.

5. *Practice compassion—with yourself.* Be patient about the progress you're making on your way to achieving your dreams. Things take time. It's easy to forget that because we live in a culture that says we can have it all (success, beauty, wealth, etc.) instantly. That only works in advertising and the movies.

6. *Keep a journal.* Write how you are feeling, what you have done or not done, what your expectations are, what is working or not working, what you wish would happen, who you need for support, etc. You can have a great dialogue with yourself in your journal. You can complain, yell, and whine there too.

7. *Do something practical. Anything!* Choose a small task you have been avoiding and complete it. Then show someone what you did. (This part is important—it brings you more endorphins!)

8. *Do something else.* If you have been struggling endlessly to contact someone to arrange a meeting, close a sale, or reach a goal and are not getting the results you want, stop! Do *not*

make another phone call! Your voice will convey your frustration (or depression). Leave the office or your house. Just do something else! And make sure it's fun—that will clear the mental cobwebs.

9. *H.A.L.T!* I love this one. It comes from a 12-step program. When you are feeling down, frustrated, or blue, ask yourself if you are:

Hungry? Then eat something.

Angry? Then deal with the anger. Don't pretend you aren't angry.

Lonely? Then call someone.

Tired? Then take a nap.

10. *Honor your body.* Eat only foods that are good for you, are wonderfully prepared, and taste fantastic. They will increase your vitality.

11. *Limit or eliminate alcohol.* If you are angry or depressed, alcohol will only make you more so.

12. *Read and listen to motivational tapes and books.* They will not only give you tips for accomplishing your goals, they will also make you feel as if you have a friend cheering you on.

13. *Reward yourself daily.* List all the things that bring you joy and include at least one in your life every day!

"In the midst of difficulty lies opportunity."
Albert Einstein

You Are Always Committing to What You Want

Sometimes we want to keep the dream as a dream and sometimes we want to make the dream real. Anxiety comes when we don't know the difference.

How about you? What is it you say you want? What would life be like for you if you actually had what it is that you say you want? How would it be different? Has your dream become a burden that you carry around with you? Do you say you want to be an entrepreneur, artist, writer, etc., only to discover that you really don't want the risk involved or the time it would take away from other parts of your life? Then you are committed to having more leisure time and feeling safe. There are no right or wrong, good or bad answers to these questions. However, making the distinction between which dreams you want to keep as dreams and which you want to make real allows you to create what it is you really want to have in your life. It lets you know which things you are willing to work for.

Aunt Bea had always wanted a Jeep. She had said so since I could remember. When she and my uncle discussed buying a new car, she'd wistfully say, "Oh, I'd love to have a Jeep. I know I'd look silly in it, but someday I'd love to have one." Four years ago she was ready for another car, and we encouraged her to buy her dream car. "Aunt Bea," we said, "just do it. You deserve your Jeep. You've always wanted one and now's the time." She was 70, her husband had died 10 years earlier (so he could no longer be the excuse), and she could afford one. "Oh, I'm too old," she said. "I'd look foolish." She bought herself a large shiny new Buick.

Aunt Bea liked the *idea* of a Jeep. She didn't want to *have* one. She was committed to looking good and not appearing silly.

What are you committed to? If you are committed to having a great job, you will do the work to find one (see Chapter 8). If you are committed to looking good; being right, safe, victimized, unhappy; or complaining, then you will do that too. If you really want to have that book published, you'll spend your spare time writing. That may mean you will not have time for other interests, socializing, playing, or watching TV.

Try This:

List 10 things that you want. Then prioritize them by comparing each one against the others. (Compare #1 against #2, #3,

#4, #5, etc.; then #2 against #3, #4, #5, etc.) The benefit of this exercise is that it doesn't let you fool yourself. The order you list them in will make no difference.

Example:

Here are Lisa's wants:

1. Make a lot of money
2. Have own business
3. Have time for friends
4. Write a book
5. Vacation in Italy
6. Find a mate
7. Learn Italian
8. Volunteer
9. Be physically fit
10. Run a marathon

Lisa asked herself, "What is more important for me today, 1 or 2?, 1 or 3?, 1 or 4?, etc., and checked which ones were more important. She then compared 2 to 3, 2 to 4, 2 to 5, etc.; then 3 to 4, 3 to 5, 3 to 6. At the end she tallied her check marks and put them in order of importance. This is what she found:

1.	Make a lot of money	✓ ✓ ✓ ✓
2.	Have own business	✓ ✓ ✓ ✓ ✓ ✓
3.	Have time for friends	✓ ✓ ✓
4.	Write a book	✓ ✓ ✓ ✓ ✓ ✓ ✓
5.	Vacation in Italy	✓ ✓ ✓ ✓ ✓
6.	Find a mate	✓ ✓ ✓ ✓
7.	Learn Italian	✓ ✓ ✓
8.	Volunteer	✓ ✓ ✓
9.	Be physically fit	✓ ✓ ✓ ✓ ✓ ✓ ✓ ✓
10.	Run a marathon	

Lisa saw that her real commitments were to being physically fit, writing a book, having her own business, and vacationing in Italy. Making a large amount of money was not her driving motivator as she had once thought and she could let go of needing to run a marathon. She also saw that finding a mate could wait until after she went to Italy. Or maybe she'd meet him there!

Respect Procrastination

"For every time there is a season."
Ecclesiastes

Procrastination is resistance with a time frame of forever. Are you really procrastinating or is this just not the right time? And if not now, when? Honor procrastination, it serves and protects you. Procrastination keeps you from committing, failing, choosing, being disappointed, or looking bad. It protects you from possibly losing friends, mates, homes, comfort levels; being wrong; looking foolish or stupid; risk, harm; being laughed at; and going broke. It may also keep you from making money, getting what you want, feeling proud, loving freely, and having joy.

If you were actually doing work that you loved, what would you complain about?

Try These:

On a clean sheet of paper, write about an activity you have been procrastinating about.

1. What are the benefits of not doing this activity? How does procrastinating serve you?
2. What would happen if you did what you have been resisting doing? What else?

3. Commit to either doing something you have been procrastinating about within the next week or not doing it ever. Then move on.

Write an Affirmation

Visualizations + affirmations + intention + action = miracles

For years athletes and salespeople around the world have been using visualization techniques and writing affirmations to reach their goals. I have used this practice to create the results I wanted in my life and have shared them with my kids, friends, clients, and total strangers. My children visualized themselves into trips to Europe, universities, scholarships, and great jobs. A diplomat I met in Paris called me six months after I taught him this technique to say the move he had wanted (that had seemed unlikely) happened exactly as he had written it! Another client wanted a new job, wrote an affirmation describing the qualities he was looking for, and the exact date by which he wanted to start—and he got it!

The most important step to creating what you want is to visualize it clearly in your mind's eye. Close your eyes and see yourself being in that setting, doing what it is you want to be doing, with the feelings you want to be experiencing. Notice the colors around you, the sounds, and the details. Relax into this picture for a few moments. When you are ready, gently open your eyes and write what you have just seen and felt as if it is still happening. Write it in the present tense beginning with the word *I*. After you have jotted this down, write your affirmation. Here is the formula:

I + Present Tense Verb + Feeling + What + Where + With

The affirmation must be stated in the positive. For example, don't say, "I'm not going to hate my job anymore." Instead try, "I am happy doing work that I love with interesting, supportive people at the salary that I need in a growing company that is located in the mountains."

Here are some examples of affirmations that came true:

"I am excited working and traveling with dynamic people creating global programs around the world." (This was one of mine.)

"I feel psyched windsurfing in the Colombia Gorge this summer." (This was one of my son's when he was in college.)

"I feel proud and excited in my new job as vice president of operations for a midsize manufacturing company in Houston, Texas." (This one came from a client.)

After you have written your affirmation, write it again on three 3" × 5" notecards. Place one in your wallet or purse, one in your office where you can easily see it, and one on the nightstand beside your bed. (If the words are too self-revealing and make you uncomfortable, create symbols or code words for them.) Read this card before you go to sleep and the first thing in the morning before you get out of bed. Refer to the one in your wallet twice during the day. It is important that when you read your affirmation, you re-create the feeling and vision you had when you first wrote it—as if it is happening now. You will also start to notice synchronistic events or information that will support what you have written. Affirmations work because of the intention you put behind them.

When you are clear about your intention and focus your energy and actions on the results you want, miracles happen.

Try These:

1. Ask yourself, "What is my intention for today? What do I want to happen today that will move me closer to my goal?"
2. Visualize what you want to happen and continue to visualize it.

   Example:

   I visualize my appointment book filled and my bank balances high. I am sitting in my beautiful office writing my next book. I feel animated and alive.

3. Create a practice affirmation with a time frame. It need not be important. Choose anything.

   Example:

   I feel light and relaxed having a clean closet where I can find things on/or before [date of your choice].

4. Now write an affirmation for a goal that is very important to you. Since goals must have a time frame, select a real date and attach it to your affirmation. Put it on your calendar.

   I am_____

   on or before _____.

5. Practice visualization by imagining that you find a parking space on the crowded street you want to park on.
6. Illustrate your desire with pictures. Collect or create visual images of your goals. If your goal is a new job, collect pictures and brochures that mirror what you will be doing. If it is a new house, car, or vacation, do the same. Put these pictures on the refrigerator, on your mirror, or on bulletin boards. See yourself doing your dream, being there. Then watch your goal show up.

7. Tape your affirmation. Record it onto a tape recorder and play it to yourself while you are driving to work. This is a great way to stay psyched and on track!

8. Recommit 500 percent to your goal.

9. Focus, focus, focus. As coaches say, "Keep your eye on the ball." That means stay focused and keep acting.

10. Take one more step. Every ministep brings you closer to your dream.

Take MiniSteps

Q: How do you eat an elephant?
A: One bite at a time.

One of the reasons video games are so popular is because they provide instant feedback. Kids of all ages spend hours playing them. They know immediately what their score is, what they've won, and who is the hero. It doesn't really matter to them if they lose, they'll start another game. Do the same with your goals. Treat them like a video game. (It would be great if jobs and schools took this lesson! They'd always have motivated employees and students.) For example, if your objective is to have a new career, break this down into easy tasks that take one hour or less to accomplish.

Sam's goal was to become a master woodworker and have his own woodworking business. He had spent years in a publishing career, but had left his previous management job to do freelance publishing work. He wanted the time he needed to pursue his dream. He had no problem finding assignments. He was very conscientious and knew his business. At the same time he was making this important career shift, he was also getting married and moving across the country. Let's look at an outline of Sam's ministeps to his goal.

Sam's Goal: Become a Master Woodworker and Have My Own Business

I. Tasks

A. Create my vision: I am a master woodworker with my own business. I am creating artfully designed and crafted furnishings that are sought after by a large clientele. I have a workroom in the barn behind my house. I love being close to my wife and children and also having time to hike and read. We have warm, loving, safe, and supportive relationships together. I have a small circle of close friends and family who are an important part of my life here. I am content and happy.

B. Pay bills. Find contract work in Oregon to pay bills. This needs to be done two months prior to leaving for Oregon.

   1. Research publishing companies there.

      a. Spend one hour at library. Ask reference librarian to help.

      b. Buy Oregon newspapers.

   2. Network, make phone calls/E-Net (one hour/day).

      a. Make list of contacts (one hour).

      b. Call five people from contact list and ask them who they know who works in those companies (one hour). (See Chapter 8.)

      c. Call references from contact list and ask them questions (one hour). (As Sam didn't know his exact moving date, he wasn't going to arrange meetings until he was sure.)

      d. Send follow-up/thank-you note (under one hour).

      e. Call another contact, etc.

C. I am a master woodworker.

   1. Contact master woodworkers in Oregon.

      a. Call cousin who has own woodworking business; ask him who he knows that I could speak with (one hour or less).

    b. Network (one hour).
  2. Enroll in woodworking classes.
    a. Research schools.
    b. Call and ask for information and applications to be sent.
    c. Network to verify quality of schools.
    d. Read information.
    e. Enroll in one class for the fall.
  3. Look for part-time work with master woodworkers when in Oregon.
D. Find housing in Oregon.
  1. Read real estate listings of Oregon papers.
  2. Talk to cousin about most desirable areas, rents, etc.

Sam's plan allowed him to move toward his goal in easily manageable steps. As he accomplished each task, he felt increasingly psyched. Every step he took brought him closer to his dream.

Try These:

1. Create a plan where you break your goals into ministeps that can be accomplished in less than one hour. Cross them off as you complete them. (Crossing off what you have accomplished releases endorphins—note the difference in how you feel!)
2. At the beginning of each month, write the five most important things to be done this month in the areas of
    work (both tasks and relationships)
    school
    family, children
    friends (close, old, new)
    home
    spiritual development
    physical and emotional well-being
    quality of life

Make sure you break them into easily manageable steps. Every day do something from each list and reward yourself for completing it.

Get Support—Form an Action Group
Don't Do It Alone

"Isolation is a dream killer."
Barbara Sher

When I was growing up I believed I needed to do everything by myself. Self-reliance was goodness. I thought not asking for help showed how capable I was. The messages I heard were: "Don't ask for help," "There must be something wrong with you if someone helps you get a job. You should do it on your own merit!"—as if asking for help meant you weren't qualified! What nonsense! Life is hard enough. No one ever does anything alone. We are all interdependent; we need each other to move forward in our lives.

I knew when I started my business that I wanted support. I had read Barbara Sher's wonderful books *WishCraft* and *Teamworks*. I decided I would follow her advice and start a support group. I looked for people in different fields (who were not doing what I was doing) and started a group we called the Vision to Action Team. We were each other's champions as well as representatives in the world. We committed to bring back new contacts and information to our meetings.

There are business/networking groups in most communities today. Or you can form your own. Put a small ad in the local newspaper: "Networking support group being formed." Or put a notice up on public bulletin boards and tell your friends, colleagues, or relatives what you are doing. Invite them to join.

Try These:

For your group to be effective:

1. *Invite people of different occupations and interests.* Each person will bring a varied network and a different way of looking at the world. Ask people who don't do what you do.
2. *Meet once every week or two.* If you meet less frequently, the dynamic momentum will stall and comfortable inertia will rear its head again.
3. *At the first meeting explain what you want to do and brainstorm ideas.* (See Chapter 3.)
4. *Divide the amount of time by the number of people.* For example, if there are six people meeting for an hour and a half, you will have 20 minutes each. Assign someone to be timekeeper. Structure the meetings around (a) updates—what you want and/or what you have done since the last time, (b) where you need help, (c) brainstorming, and (d) what you commit to do for the next meeting.
5. *At the end of the first meeting each person must commit to doing something on his or her list of ideas that the group generated.* At the following meeting you will report back on what you accomplished, what you tried to do and couldn't, and what you didn't get to. The others will then help you decide whether you should continue in the same way or try another idea. This is your accountability team, your support group; they are your extra ears and your champions.

Each member of the team has ties to the world and is out there supporting you. They will think of you when they hear of something you might be interested in—new leads, new contacts, and new information. They will prod you on and help heal your wounds. They will encourage you and laugh with you. You will have created a little community that will help you reach those dreams that you really want. Remember, we all need each other. It is too hard to do it alone!

Program Your Body to Revitalize Your Mind

We have limited power over our own minds. The mind, after all, is always thinking, planning, assessing, projecting, etc. It is almost impossible *not* to think. Thoughts come and go and continually affect our feelings. They often seem to have a life of their own and always influence physical reactions. For example, think of a lemon. Close your eyes and imagine the bright yellow color, the oval shape, the sweet smell and sour citrus taste of a lemon. Imagine yourself drinking the lemon juice straight from the lemon. Now what did you experience? Did your mouth pucker? Were you able to almost taste the sourness? And all because you *thought* about eating a lemon!

You do the same when you think of something that makes you angry or excited—your heart will race and your palms will sweat. When you think of something sad, you become sad, sometimes even to the point of tears. When you are anxious about your next appointment or meeting, your stomach might become upset, your shoulders may stiffen. Suddenly you have a headache. Or perhaps you simply don't feel as *up* as you would like.

Try This:

Try programming your body to shift your feelings. Here is a technique to change your mood by just snapping your fingers: Stand with your feet placed firmly on the floor about 6 to 8 inches apart (directly under your hips). Your shoulders are relaxed (bring them down from your ears), your back is straight, and your arms are by your sides. Now think of a time when you felt *great*. It might have been a time when you knew you had the answer, or when you were really good at what you were doing. It might have been when the person you were with really liked you, or when you were feeling really self-confident (like the first time you were able to ride that two-wheeler without any help. Remember that time?). Now snap your fingers. Once more remember that time when you felt so terrific and snap your fingers. While you snap, say (either aloud or to yourself), "I feel great!" Relax. Walk around the room a little and do the procedure again. Repeat this five to ten times, relaxing and walking around between repetitions. You are in the process of anchoring that great feeling into your body. So the next time you *don't* feel great, all you have to do is snap your fingers and you *will*. If your family or housemates think you are weird doing this, teach them how to do it too. (Or practice in the bathroom.)

Make Being Uncomfortable *More* Uncomfortable!

"Failure is not an option."

> Gene Kranz as played by Ed Harris, *Apollo 13*

"Most people cannot and will not change unless financial, physical, emotional, and spiritual ruin forces them to."

> John Long, *Writer's Little Book of Wisdom*

In the motivational race between pleasure and pain, pain wins.

What motivates us to change is either the pursuit of pleasure or the avoidance of pain. Research has shown that the latter is the stronger motivator. Those of us who stay in painful jobs, bad relationships, and unhealthy behavioral patterns do so because we fear something worse will happen if we act differently. We don't wake up in the morning and think, "Let's see how miserable I can be today." We subconsciously believe the old myth that the devil you know is better than the devil you don't. We become comfortable with our discomfort, rationalize it, and remain in it. Our only hope for breaking this self-defeating pattern is to make our discomfort so painful that we will do almost anything to change. Since we are already experts at worrying and "awfulizing" (creating imaginary disasters), change should be easy!

The president of Tony's company called me to coach Tony when they laid him off. Tony had been a senior contributor whom the president had hired. He just "hadn't worked out." When I met Tony, he was very dejected. This was not the first time he had been laid off. He had an MBA, was a hard worker, and said he had been committed to doing a good job for *all* the companies he had worked for. Yet he usually didn't remain longer than two years with any one of them. Tony's self-esteem had hit bottom and he didn't want to go through this again. He had also just turned 50 and was afraid his age would work against him on his next job search.

As I got to know Tony, I saw that he was personable, smart, and highly entertaining. It was clear that he hadn't been doing work that matched his talents and personality no matter how hard he tried. Tony didn't want to leave companies every two years. He wanted a secure job that would last his lifetime. Most of his career had been spent in administration and operations. Since he was always recovering from the previous layoff or trying to fit into a new job, Tony had never spent the necessary time to discover what type of environment would support who he was. He no longer knew what he was good at and doubted himself. With his job history, it was no wonder! After a few sessions Tony uncovered what he really loved doing: performing, making people laugh, training, and working with personal computers. His most satisfying work experiences had been when he was helping others learn a software program and when he was fixing technical problems. He also told me he had enjoyed playing guitar and telling jokes in coffeehouses when he was younger. He loved being in front of an audience. He thought about doing training where he could use his business, teaching, and stage skills. Tony started networking and taking steps to market himself as a training consultant for PCs and business software. His major hurdle was that he *hated* marketing. He was uncomfortable talking to people on the phone, asking for help, and selling himself. However, he *hated more* the thought of being broke and finding and losing another job. He saw himself becoming destitute, unloved, without friends, and a bagman—on the streets in his old age—if he didn't take the steps now. Little by little he started finding assignments, building his business, and attracting more clients. Today he is a successful PC software training consultant. And he still hates marketing himself.

Try This:

State what it is you want to do. Write it down. Then state what will happen if you don't take action to accomplish what it is you want. If you remain doing what you are now doing and feeling what you are now feeling forever, what is the worst possible situation that will occur? And then what? How will it affect your relationships, your health, and your self?

If you keep doing what you've done, you'll keep getting what you've got. Being scared and feeling like a fraud is part of the process.

> "Feel the fear and do it anyway."
> Susan Jeffers

Ask for Guidance

In my many career changes, I always seemed to be on a continuous highway that went in a loop between a place called

Despair and a town called Action. I didn't simply visit these places, I resided inside them. If I was in Action, I would accomplish more in three days than most people do in one month. I would call 100 people, send out 40 letters, set up 15 appointments, plan a new project, clean up correspondence, pay my bills, and go for a walk. However, if I was closer to Despair, I would feel overwhelmed, paralyzed, and unable to see my way out. Ready to give up, I would remember what my friend Colquit said, "Ask the Universe to give you a sign that you are on the right path. Also notice the signs you have already received." I would ask and try to muddle through the rest of the day. Later the phone would ring and I'd find that someone was calling to see if I'd be interested in doing a new project. Or I would receive a note from a client acknowledging how much I had helped him or her. Or it would be a reporter who wanted to quote me and send a photographer out. Coincidence? Maybe.

I love the story of the man who was sailing his new 50-foot sailboat to Bermuda when he got caught in a hurricane. Gale winds were blowing and waves were crashing over the boat. The man prayed to God that the storm would subside and he would be able to save his boat. A freighter came by to take him off his sailboat. He said, "No, no thanks, God will save me and my boat." He knew if he were rescued, he would have to leave his boat to the sea. He prayed again for clear weather. A few hours later, a Coast Guard ship came by. "Do you want to be rescued?" the captain asked. "No thanks," came the reply. "I'll just wait it through." Then the Coast Guard sent a helicopter and radioed that the storm had become dangerous. Again the man refused help. He knew God would save him. The storm indeed got worse, his boat capsized, and he drowned. At the Pearly Gates he said to God, "What happened? I prayed to you. You were supposed to save me." God answered, "What do you mean? I sent you two ships and a helicopter!"

Observe what is given and take what you get.

The Universe is a great teacher. Sometimes the marketplace is one of its messengers. If you are working too much and are continually unsuccessful, there is something wrong. If you are struggling and not succeeding, stop and reflect. You may need to change direction. Ask yourself how else you might approach this problem in a way that might be easier. (See Chapter 3.) Or is this field really right for you after all?

Try These:

1. How have you been supported in being where you are today?
2. What signs have you received in the past indicating that you were on the right track, or on the wrong one?
3. Ask the Universe for guidance now and pay attention when the guidance shows up.

8

Choose Your Tactics

You always have choices.

You Are in Charge

Are you ready for your perfect job? Be clear and own your power!

Most of us hate to look for work. Period. We want the great job to knock on our front door and say "I'm here. I'm just what you want, I'll make you very successful, you won't have to worry about a thing, and you can live happily ever after." It's the Job Charming fantasy again.

Most of us also hate to market ourselves. The Inner Critic whispers loudly:

"I shouldn't have to."

"They should know how valuable I am by the work I do."

"It's not nice to talk about myself."

"I'll look foolish."

"They'll think I'm boasting and conceited."

"It feels sleazy."

"Those aren't my skills."

"This culture doesn't support it."

"They won't like/value me if I do."

"I'm too busy."

"Salespeople do that and you know what *they're* like!"

"I just don't want to."

It's no wonder so many people bury their heads in want ads and spend countless hours responding to ads, even though only a small percentage of all jobs come from this method. To many, the image of selling is so onerous that they will do almost anything to avoid picking up the phone and marketing themselves. However, when I ask them to describe salespeople with whom they like to do business, they say those salespeople are "informative, honest, thorough, attentive, good at following through, service-oriented, and nonpressuring." In other words, just like they are!

People won't know who you are and how you can help them unless you tell them. Having work you love is all about sharing who you are with the world. Here are some insights I have learned both from personal experience and from interviewing thousands of people over the years.

Interviewing Tips

- *Beware of jerks.* Yes, they can show up in interviews. If someone asks inappropriate questions, is rude, or is uncomfortably confrontational, ask yourself if you really want to work with that person. Does he or she represent the culture of the company or is this just one person's individual style? Perhaps the person is just having a bad day. Make sure you meet at least three people in the company before signing on. If you accept the job, you accept the culture and you will be part of it.
- *Help people interview you.* Most people don't know how to interview. It's your role to help them. When someone asks you, "What would you do if . . . ," answer with "What I did in a similar case was to . . . ," and relate a situation you had either at work, in the community, in your hobbies/interests, or at home and how you successfully dealt with it. Keep in mind that the interviewer posed a theoretical question that did not allow you to tell what you did. (This is a very poor interviewing technique, which is too frequently used.) Your answer will give an example of your skills based on an event that actually happened. We remember stories. The way people behaved in the past is the *only* evidence we have of how they will behave in the future.
- *You always make an impression.* Most people walk around as if they are invisible. How you dress, your posture, vitality, personal hygiene, haircut, voice, and language reflect not only what you think of yourself but also what you think of others. (Sloppiness says "You're not worth looking good for.") This is true not only in an interview but also in the supermarket or anywhere else where you could meet a potential contact.

*There is so little we can actually control in our lives.
Sometimes it is limited to what we put on and in our bodies
and minds.*

- *Don't say "I'm looking for a job."* This is a burden for the person you say it to. People want to help you, but this type of comment makes them feel responsible for finding you that job. They may wish they could tell you about the right position, but often they don't know how and consequently they feel powerless and embarrassed that they can't. (Don't you also want to help when you are asked?) Instead say, "I want to connect with people who work in a dynamic, fast-growing company where there is a lot of opportunity, or one in the _____ business. Who do you know who works in this type of company?" Or you might say, "I want to connect with people who are responsible for marketing for a dynamic, fast-growing company (or with a small, two- to three-person shop), etc." Then your contacts will more likely be able to give you information that will be useful to you in your search.
- *Don't waste your time or anyone else's.* If you aren't interested in the job or it isn't the right client for you, say so. Perhaps you know someone for whom it might be the perfect fit. Spend your time and energy getting the *right* offer.
- *Don't take a job with a company that is willing to hire you on the spot.* Insist on meeting other people and interview them. Remember, if they hire you immediately, they'll fire you immediately too. Ask about what training and support you will receive.
- *All you need is one.* You are only looking for *one* job. And that will be the best one for *you*, one where you can make a contribution and succeed.
- *Ask for what you really want!* State your goal in a clear, concise manner. "I would like the names of contacts who would be good prospects for my business. My ideal client is the _____. Who could you refer me to?"

- *Broadcast to the world what it is you do!* Marketing and promotions are based on the simple truth that you need to inform
  people of your product or service so that they can buy it. You
  can have the best widget in existence, but if you don't tell
  anyone about it, nobody will benefit from it!

Do Your Market Research the Easy Way

There are two main areas of support that are indispensable:

1. The reference librarians at your local library or universities
2. Your friends

Reference librarians are the best-kept-secret resource
around. They are trained to know where and how to find information. Tell them what you are looking for in any part of the
world and they will help you locate it.

Your friends will be able to direct you to people they know
who can give you the unpublished info on a company's culture,
management style, the kinds of people working there, what
customers think of their products and services, positives and
negatives of working there, etc. A referral is also your best
introduction. Much better than alumni lists or cold calling—
although don't rule these out either. Simply approach your
friends and their referrals first and meet with them if at all
possible. Real relationships are not built over phone lines or
computer networks. They can be *continued* electronically, but it
is face-to-face contact that will cement them.

Research Tips

- *Want ads are part of your market research.* Although only a small
  percentage of all jobs are found through answering classi-

fieds, want ads do provide you with a wealth of information about which companies are expanding. Use them as part of your networking data when you are prospecting for clients or job hunting.

- *Identify your allies—both current and past.* Your real wealth is not only in your skills and experience but also in the people you know. They include those who can vouch for you and who want to see you succeed. Make a list of present and former:

  managers
  colleagues
  employees
  customers
  vendors
  friends
  neighbors
  town, state, and federal government
  relatives
  anyone you've written a check to in the past year
    (your hairdresser/barber and dentist have an
    incredible network!)

Recruiters Are Salespeople

Recruiters are *not* career counselors. They often get a bad rap because of applicants' unrealistic expectations. Their income is based on finding qualified candidates for client companies who *pay* them. By all means use (but don't abuse) them. In fact, try to develop a long-term relationship with one or two reliable recruiters. They should be part of your career resources. Ask your friends or colleagues for names of recruiters they have worked with and trust. Professional headhunters have worked hard to gain their good reputations. (And, yes, there are some you want to avoid at all costs. Listen to your gut. If you are the least bit uncomfortable with the person's style or behavior, run, don't walk, for the door.)

Recruiters, employment agencies, and executive search companies look for people who fit current openings: square pegs into square holes, round pegs into round ones. In general, they cannot help you if you are changing careers.

How to Get Over the Networking Jitters

The remarkable thing about working in today's world of downsizing, reengineering, high risk, lack of stability, and FUD (fear, uncertainty, and doubt) is that *everyone is in the same boat.* The good news is that we have become more compassionate, more giving of our time and knowledge, and more willing to listen and help. We do this because it is the right thing to do and also because we don't know when we too will be asking for help. Every time we connect with a new person we increase our network (or potential community) and theirs as well. Look around. The world has become smaller and warmer.

Picking up the phone and calling strangers may not be one of your favorite activities. To help yourself feel more comfortable, identify what it is that you want to accomplish *before* you pick up the phone or meet with them.

Try This:

- Don't make your first call a cold call. Make it a warm call. Allow yourself at least one month to call only referrals— people who have been referred to you by friends, people you know well and trust. (After the one-month period, you will be ready to call anyone.)
- To get referrals, you need only *one* person to open you up to the world. Help people help you. Be clear.

The formula for preparing the initial question for your friends is this:

1. State what you do.
2. State who you want to connect with. You might identify a position, a skill, someone who works in xyz company, or who works and/or lives in a certain part of the country/world, etc.
3. Ask who your friend might know who does the kind of work you are interested in or who might know someone who does. Ask your friend whether you can use his or her name when you call the referral.
4. If nothing comes of the referral, you've lost nothing. But the right referral could result in contacts, new relationships, and new friends.

Here is an example of a conversation I have with friends when I want to meet new people:

"Hi, Ron, this is Cheryl. Perhaps you can help me. As you know, I lead motivational seminars and coach people to help them have work that they love. I'm interested in connecting with people in small to large companies. Who do you know who is a VP of human resources or sales or a ceo or president I could talk to? I want to meet them, get to know them, and let them know me and what I do."

This is not a ruse. I may have just the service that will support their needs or those of the people they refer me to. If they don't know me and what I do, and trust me, they won't be able to use my services. We want to do business with people we trust, and trust takes time. This first conversation is potentially the beginning of a long relationship.

Here is a sample conversation with a new contact:

CHERYL: Hello. My name is Cheryl Gilman and Ron Jones suggested I call you. I'm networking and Ron said you'd be a good person to talk to. I coach and lead seminars that help people have work that they love. I'd like to meet you and give us a chance to get to know each other in the event you might be interested in my services at some time.

CONTACT: Sure, that sounds fine. How do you know Ron? [The conversation continues and we set up a time to meet.]

Networking is building relationships, asking for advice or help, and *giving back*. Every new person you meet is an addition to your community and *you to theirs*. During the conversations you have with your new contacts, don't forget to ask how you can help them. We are all here to support each other. And if you are out in the world networking, you may have some information or contacts that they can use too. Have fun and enjoy the process. People want you to succeed and they are also willing to help. Aren't you willing to do the same?

Networking Tips

- Consistently ask, "Who do you know who . . . ?" Make a list of clients and friends from whom you can ask for referrals and support. Call at least one a day. Follow up on leads immediately. Also ask your clients and friends, "What do you need and how can I help?"
- Join and work for two associations: one with people from whom you can learn (who do what you do or what you want to do) and one where the members might be able to use your services (where there aren't a lot of you there!). Don't pay dues until you have attended at least three meetings and are sure the association supports your objectives. (This counsel comes from lots of learning experiences!)
- Make cold calls. You don't always need an introduction. Sometimes it's faster and more effective to simply call the person with whom you want to connect. You may have read or heard about them in newspapers or by word of mouth.
- Do your homework. Familiarize yourself with the industry, organization, and generally known issues before you warm or cold call. Use newspapers, magazines, your library, or the Internet to obtain your information.

How to Get the Appointment You Want

You will encounter resistance. So what?

Before you pick up the phone, first determine your intention to have that appointment. If you are committed to your goal and this meeting will potentially support your objective, speak with a sense of urgency. Act as if your life depends on it. (Sometimes it feels as though it does.) And visualize yourself meeting with the person you're contacting.

Expect a Screener

This is the person or technology that keeps you from reaching the person you want to speak to. If the screener is a human being, develop a relationship with him or her and ask for help. Let the person know how important it is for you to speak with so and so, and ask for the best time to do that. Explain who referred you and that your contact said so and so would be the best person to speak with. Mention that you only need a few minutes of so and so's time. Write down the screener's name so that when you call back and try again you can address him or her personally. Knowing someone's name is a first step in developing a relationship. If the screener can't connect you with so and so, ask, "Who else should I speak with? This is very important to me." (Don't say "Is there anyone else I can speak with?" You want to avoid asking questions that can elicit a "no" response.)

If the screener is an answering device or voice-mail system, leave messages until someone calls you back. Repeat your name and number at the beginning and end of your recording. Call at off hours—before work or later in the day. If your efforts to connect with the person are using too much of your energy, move on. It's obvious that this isn't the right person. Find someone else—someone higher in the organization or in another organization. Just move on.

Tip

No doesn't need to mean forever. We respond to *no* as if it were the *last* word. Believing this may have been crucial to our survival when we were children but it no longer applies. *No* is only a word. Just because the answer is *no* today does not mean it will be the same next week or next month. The naysayer may need your services by then.

Give a Choice of Two

This is a sales tip I have found helpful whether setting up meetings or negotiating with my kids. The advice allowed me to choose the parameters. The magic number is two, not three. Three choices are one too many—too much thinking is required.

For an appointment ask, "Which is better for you—this week or next week?" If neither works, look at your calendar and offer, "How about the week after that or at the end of the month?" Once you have narrowed down the week, ask, "Early in the week or later in the week?" Then, if early, "Monday or Tuesday?" Then, "Morning or afternoon?" "At 9:00 or 11:00?" If the person is really busy and can't fit you in during normal business hours, suggest an early breakfast meeting or an appointment right after work. Continuing this dialog shows your commitment to meeting with the person. It also shows that you are a determined go-getter. And you haven't even been to the appointment yet!

Tip

• You can use the Choice of Two technique with family and friends to choose movies, restaurants, bedtime, etc. You not only get what you want but you also help them decide.

Your One-Minute Intro

Remember—this is your show!

One of the most commonly asked questions in an interview is, "Tell me about yourself." I used to hate this question. My internal voices would cry out, "What do they mean?" "What do they really want to know?" "How should I answer this—what part of my life should I talk about and is this going to be the right answer?" as I'd babble something that would give away my confusion. Over the years I developed a technique that allowed me to say briefly what I wanted the interviewer to know and not put them to sleep or waste their time or my own. It was also the springboard for further questions.

When I was thinking about starting my business, I called a networking friend for contacts in the outplacement business. I told her I was interested in meeting with presidents of major firms in the Boston area and asked whom she knew. I asked if I could use her name. She said I could. I then phoned the contacts, told them who had referred me, and mentioned that I would like to meet with them and explore outplacement opportunities. They all agreed to see me.

Once again, I was thinking about doing something I hadn't been trained for while there were hundreds of qualified people looking for the same assignments. Most people in this industry are counselors, psychologists, ministers, or social workers. They have degrees in career counseling, or they've had experience in human resources or training. I didn't fit any of those models.

Before my meetings, I thought about which of my skills might be interesting to a president of an outplacement firm when they said, "Tell me about yourself." In the response I used I emphasized my management, sales, and teaching skills as well as my recruiting background—all qualities that could be useful in leading outplacement seminars as well as in attracting new clients. Talking about anything else in my career(s) would have diluted my purpose. Here's my one-minute intro (and, yes, I did get a contract with one of the companies).

"For the past five years I've been a senior manager leading global change programs for xyz company. Most of my experience before that had been in sales and marketing with recruiting products: from having my own employment consulting business to agency work to account management for a recruitment software product in the early '80s. I'm from this area, grew up in Framingham—when it was cow country—live in Belmont now and have two grown kids I'm very proud of. I have a bachelor's degree in languages—speak French and Spanish, and taught in a previous career. I'm exploring outplacement companies in the area and really appreciate your meeting with me."

Try creating a script for your one-minute intro. On a clean sheet of paper rewrite the following, filling in the blanks as you go.

I am a _____ (how you describe yourself).
  OR
I've been _____ (state what in your past you can relate to how you currently describe yourself).
Most of my background has been in _____ as well as _____.
I went to school at _____
  AND/OR
Most of my (formal/informal) education has been in

_____.

I'm originally from, grew up in, and/or live in

_____.

I'm exploring or am interested in learning more about

_____.

One-Minute Intro Tips

- *Don't use the word* expert *to describe yourself.* Experts don't need to. People who are the most expert are the most humble and the most open. The powerful people (that you will like) are not the same as power-motivated people. They don't have to try to appear important—they already are.

- *Avoid stories!* Don't elaborate during your one-minute intro. That can come later. What you say here is a springboard for more conversation. Again, you are helping the person who is interviewing you.
- *The less you say, the more powerful you appear.* Keep your statements brief and to the point. Ask questions.

Make Them Feel Safe

"When I listen I have the power,
When I speak I give it away."

François-Marie Voltaire

People hire people whom they trust and who make them feel safe. The purpose for any first interview or sales call is to begin a relationship—*not* to sell something or get an offer. We buy from people we trust and trust takes time. We forget that in our "get the results quick" culture, it takes at least five contacts for people to trust you. Your first goal in an interview is to make others feel comfortable with *you*.

Interviewing Tips

- *Make them feel comfortable.* Establish rapport. Ask how the person knows the person who referred you, etc. Notice something in his or her office—a picture, books, etc.—and comment on it. Find some commonality if possible.
- *Say yes to coffee.* Or tea or water. If the person you are meeting with offers you something to drink, say yes—even if you don't want it. You don't have to drink it. It allows the interviewer to give you something, which brings you into their energy sphere. An alternative is to say, "Yes, if you are."

- *Mirror the other person.* Match their speech patterns and body language. If the person you are speaking with is a laid-back schmoozer, don't rush him. On the other hand, if she talks quickly and is impatient for results and answers, try speaking at a quicker rate.
- *Sit up straight.* Don't slouch or lean back with your hands clasped behind your head. It will either convey arrogance or sloth.
- *Ask coaching questions.* "What is your biggest challenge?" "If you could have it (your company, product, this situation, etc.) any way you wanted it, how would that look?" You don't have to have the answers.
- *Listen.* Be curious, not smart.
- *Ask for a business card before you leave.* Again this allows the interviewer to give you something. It also provides you with the correct spelling of their name and title for when you send your thank-you note.
- *Send a thank-you note within 48 hours.* This can be handwritten or typed. Keep it brief. You might refer to information that you found particularly interesting or helpful. If the person has given you the name of someone else to call, mention the status of that call or meeting and thank them. If a proposal is warranted, that will take more time and can be sent later. Every time you connect with someone—by phone, mail, or in person—you strengthen that relationship. Sincerity is important too.

Allow Room for Flow

Do practice; don't overprepare.

There are times when I'm searching for something or someone (e.g., the right answer, person, or situation) that things just happen as if by magic. I call this being in the flow. *Flow* means spontaneity, creative thinking, chemistry, and being yourself. It happens when you meet someone whose philosophy is in sync with yours and with whom you envision yourself working because it would be such fun. Flow happens when you can look someone in the eye and say, "I want to work with you. When can I start?" and you mean it. Flow happens when you are working on a team and there is an electricity, an exciting energy that is moving everyone forward. Everyone is jumping in with new ideas and making commitments, and time flies.

It is relatively easy to prepare for any interview, yet it also takes some time. You can use information resources that are readily available in libraries, such as newspapers, journals, microfiche, encyclopedias of associations or consultants, Standard & Poors, Moody's, etc. There are also many excellent books on interviewing techniques, as well as coaches who will help you practice. However, I must caution you against using too many of the standard answers that are found in these books ("Q: What is your biggest weakness? A: I'm a perfectionist."). By all means, use them as guides; however, it is most important that your answers genuinely reflect you.

Enjoy the process. Treat it as a game. Here is an opportunity to meet someone new. She might even become a friend. The interviewer is facing many of the same concerns you are—he or she just happens to be sitting on the other side of the desk. The interviewer also wants support and help with his or her own problems. Your job is not only to have the answers to the interviewer's questions but also to probe and discover how you can help *him or her*. It is also a chance to allow room for flow, where you can listen for what isn't being said, where you can establish trust, and where you can let new ideas be created. That's when interviewing is fun!

Speaking of the desk, try not to sit directly across from the person interviewing you when there is a desk or large table between you. This is a position of limited power. Move your chair closer or at an angle if you can. Most people are aware of this. This may also tell you something about your interviewer's need for safety and/or control.

Try These:

The following are some questions for you to ask during an interview. Use them as triggers (sparks to generate other questions) when looking for clients, information, or a new job.

1. What issues are important to you (or your organization*)?
2. What is your biggest challenge/problem?
3. What is your (or your organization's) role or plans for . . . ?
4. How do you plan to maintain/improve that position?
5. How does the organization (your management) support you, this role (with budget/staff/training)? What is their (your) long-/short-term commitment?
6. What is the organization (department, group, individual) doing to be unique? How does it differentiate itself?
7. Who do you consider your major competition?
8. How does the organization/department sustain its uniqueness and/or improve competitiveness?
9. How does the organization treat people who have taken a risk and failed?
10. How is success measured here? How do you know when you are successful?
11. How else do I find additional information? Who would you suggest I contact? (Don't say, "Do you know anyone I can speak to?" Avoid questions where you can get a simple "no" response.)

*Organization refers to any group larger than three (e.g., department, company, staff, group, class, association, unit, order, foundation, institute, establishment, branch, division, etc.).

Provide a Service—Solve Their Problems

"Consultant a person who gives expert or professional advice."

American College Dictionary, 2nd edition

You are already a consultant.

As we discussed earlier, we are all self-employed consultants who give advice (gleaned from our experience, skills, and know-how) to our clients. These clients either hire us to be on their full- or part-time payroll, retain us for a specific time period or pay us for our services on a project basis. It is helpful to approach any job or business search as if it were a consulting assignment.

After Jack was laid off a few years ago, he narrowed his job search down to two competing companies. He networked throughout both to meet people and find out what problems these companies were facing. His ultimate goal was to connect with the presidents of these companies for a senior-level position. However, he didn't want to contact them until he had all the information he needed. He wanted them to be eager to hire him. He approached his search as if he were a consultant, only he wasn't being paid. As a consultant doing market research, he interviewed some of the employees as well as the companies' customers. He asked them what they liked and didn't like about the products and services they were receiving. He then wrote a proposal to the presidents of both companies, along with a detailed description of his findings. Of course, they wanted to see him and one of them made him an offer he couldn't refuse.

Try These:

Answer these questions:

1. How could you approach your current situation (job/career search, goal, dream, etc.) as if you were a consultant?
2. What research would you do?
3. What expertise would you draw on?
4. Who would your clients be? (Clients/customers can be people or departments within an internal or outside organization.)
5. Who would *their* customers be? Where could you find information about them? How would that be useful to your current project?

No One Wants to Read Your Resume

After reading thousands of resumes over the years and having written almost as many for others as well as myself, I have come to two conclusions:

1. Keep your resume focused on what you want to do *next*.
2. Don't send a resume unless you have to.

Don't mail or give your resume to the world. Be selective. Every time you send your resume you allow someone to pass judgment on you. If you must send mail, send brief letters indicating your interest in meeting with so and so. A resume can be a follow-up piece. Keep it professional and brief—no more than two pages. It takes a recruiter under seven seconds to read your resume and decide if you should be a candidate. Seven seconds—after you have belabored, revised, sweated, and worried over the impact of each word as if you were carving a piece of art. Send your resume out sparingly. Try to set up appointments first. Bring a copy of your resume with you or send it later as a reminder of your meeting.

Dos and Don'ts of Resume Writing

- *Don't highlight what you don't want to do.* The purpose of your resume is to tell the reader what it is you want him or her to know about you—not the *whole* truth. Not everything you've done in your lifetime. (Yes, it is impressive, but there is too much to read.) Your resume should reflect only that experience that supports what you want to do next. For example, if you want to do marketing and don't want to do administration or programming in your next job, don't highlight administration or programming. Emphasize what you did—*ever*—that was related to marketing. You are only going to get seven seconds of viewing time—give the reader all the help you can.
- *Don't put your objective on your resume.* Write it in the cover letter or tell the interviewer what it is. Having your objective on your resume will limit you. Your objective is bound to change.
- *Do start with a summary statement.* Like the executive summary section of a business plan (which few people want to read either), your resume's summary statement should highlight what the remainder of the document will say. Your summary statement should be a two- to four-sentence paragraph that emphasizes the experience, strengths, and knowledge that you want to use in your next position, even if they're not those you use now.

Jennifer had worked in marketing, management, administration, and customer service for 10 years. Although she was originally trained in graphic design, she hadn't been paid to use that skill since her first job after college 15 years earlier. She now wanted graphic design to be part of her day-to-day responsibilities.

Jennifer's Summary:
Fifteen years marketing/communications experience in finance, high-tech, and health care industries. Major strengths in creative problem-solving, graphic design, and building client relationships. Awarded Employee of the Year for increasing sales by 25 percent.

- *State how you want to be remembered in your first and last sentences.* What we see and hear first and last is what we remember.
- *Do avoid the words* responsible for. *They don't say what you did.* Use action verbs and keep it brief.
- *Do use your resume as a carrot.* Tickle the prospective employer's interest. That's all. Who you are is what is impressive. Make the reader want to get to know you better.
- *Don't send a resume if you are sending a detailed letter.* It is redundant and diminishing. You can send your resume later if there is interest.
- *Do follow your summary statement with a listing of your accomplishments.* These are three to five key accomplishments that you want to bring to the reader's attention that support what you said in your summary. Here's an example from Jennifer's resume:

Key Accomplishments:
- Developed national marketing/communications programs for major health care provider that increased enrollments by 300 percent.
- Conceived advertising campaign for major computer manufacturer that resulted in additional $2 million in sales.
- Created award-winning design campaign for major financial services organization that increased their market share by 30 percent.

Try This:

In order to write accomplishment statements as well as to remind yourself of how valuable you have been, do the following exercise. This will also help you sort out what you have really contributed so that you will be able to talk about it in an interview.

1. Describe a *problem* or *situation* that existed in a previous job or activity.
2. Tell what *action* you took to resolve that problem or situation.
3. Then say what *result* came about from this action (cost/time savings, increased productivity, sales, efficiencies, customer satisfaction, improved relations, etc.) Quantify when possible.

- *Don't be modest.* You can take credit for work that you did as part of a team. No one does it alone. You don't have to have single-handedly made $1 billion in sales for the company. Most presidents don't either. And you can take responsibility for a team's success, as can everyone else on the team.
- *Don't use superlatives.* Avoid words such as *superior, outstanding, incredible,* etc. These words sound like marketing hype. They diminish your credibility.
- *Don't use four-syllable, technical, overly erudite words or acronyms* unless you are positive that the only person reading your resume will be someone exactly like you. Assuming that everyone will understand what you're talking about will not serve you. Everyone is too busy to spend time sorting through what you are trying to say. *Keep it simple.*
- *Don't use the word* I *in your resume.* Start sentences with action verbs (e.g., *coached, led, increased, developed, designed, created, organized,* etc.).
- *Don't say "References available upon request."* That is a filler line. Of course they'll be available. (But do check with your references first and review with them what you want them to say *before* you give their names to anyone.)

- *Do proofread your resume.* It's easy to overlook minor errors—ask your friends or family to read it too.
- *Do check with others in your field for guidelines for writing resumes for your specialty.* Each discipline has its own conventions. A lawyer's resume format is different from an academic's, which is different from a salesperson's, etc.
- *Resume writing is an art, not a science.* You will get a wide variety of opinions on what your resume should look like. There are excellent reference books on writing resumes available in libraries or bookstores. Create your resume so that *you* will be happy with it. (There is also software available for both developing resumes and tracking networking contacts.)
- *And never, never lie on your resume.* It will come around to haunt you!
- *You will not be hired on the basis of your resume.* It may get you an interview. It can also be used as a leave-behind to remind someone of the great conversation they had with you.
- *Only 25 percent of all jobs are found through resumes.* The rest are found through networking. So pay attention to how much time you spend on your resume. You can put your energy to more productive use.

Write a Bio

If you are starting your own business or don't want to use a resume, a simple bio can provide a user-friendly overview of what you do. This is a very high-level sketch of the skills and experience that you want to highlight. It also offers the reader an easily digestible way to understand what you do.

A readily accessible bio can save you a lot of time. It can be used by organizations to introduce you when you speak; it can be sent to newspapers in a press release. It can also accompany articles that you write. People will read your bio, while they may groan at the thought of getting lost in your resume.

A bio can be two paragraphs that fit on the back of a brochure or it can be a full-page description typed and double-spaced. It is important to keep the language simple. Use mostly two-syllable words. Use words of three syllables or more only when you can't avoid them.

Notice brochures you receive for examples of bios. Ask yourself which ones you like. Read book jackets too. A copy of a bio I use is included at the back of this book as an example. The important part to remember is to keep it as conversational as possible—even if you are at the chairman level. Again, the reason we read bios is that they are easy, accessible, and user-friendly. Keep it simple.

9

Help Your
Kids and Friends

———❁❁❁———

"Ride the horse in the direction it's going."

Chinese proverb

Support *How* They Are

"Enrico Caruso's parents wanted him to be an
engineer. His teachers said he had no voice at all and
could not sing.

Thomas Edison's teachers said he was too stupid
to learn anything.

The sculptor Rodin's father said, 'I have an idiot
for a son.' Described as the worst pupil in the school,
Rodin failed three times to secure admittance to the
school of art. His uncle called him uneducable."

Jack Canfield and Mark Hansen,
Chicken Soup for the Soul

We want to help those we love as they struggle with decisions
for their future. Sometimes we believe our answers are the right
ones. Sometimes we're wrong.

Jack was diagnosed with attention deficit disorder (ADD) as
a child. When he was 18 he went to Johns Hopkins University
to prepare for a career as an art curator. He quickly saw that
it wasn't the right profession for him. He was interested in 14
things at the same time and couldn't sit still. He struggled
through college and graduated. He had always loved movies, so
he decided to apprentice himself to filmmakers. His parents
thought he should get a "real" job, but Jack knew that he
couldn't be in one place from nine to five and continued to
pursue filmmaking. He did not make a lot of money at first. He
cut and pasted and learned camera work and production. He
married, had a family, and started to make more money. He
started a film company and had people on payroll. It succeeded
and then tumbled. He started again, this time with a "virtual"
company. Now he hires from his broad network of friends and

colleagues when he needs help. He shoots films for groups around the world and travels to Asia and Africa and throughout North America and Europe. People he hires love to work with him because he is joyful and gives back. He is still interested in 14 things at the same time and has trouble sitting still. Had Jack gone to work for someone in a job he wasn't suited for, he might have thought there was something wrong with him for the rest of his life. He would not have been able to share his joy and his craft. How fortunate for Jack and everyone who knows him that he made the right choice.

Try This:

As you think about your children or friends, reflect on the way they are. Ask yourself what they love to do. What is their energy level and attention span? What are their interests? What makes them happy?

Don't Fix What Ain't Broken

When my son was young he often became totally committed to his passion of the moment. It was *never* school. At four years old, he would spend hours constructing boats with no bottoms out of two-by-fours in the basement and proudly shout, "Come see!" At six, the objects of his desire were vans. He collected photos of vans, drew pictures of vans, asked for plastic models, talked about vans, pointed them out on the highway, and explained their differences and benefits to all who would listen. And, of course, he wanted one. Badly. At eight, it was stereos, at fourteen, Porsches. Then more stereos, guitars, music. He took up windsurfing. He pursued all of these interests with the same ardor and commitment. School was never a priority—he managed to get by. He preferred to play, joke around with his friends, listen to music, and hang out. I didn't worry about it. I knew he would know what he needed to do.

Even as a kid, Adam's ultimate goal was "to make a lot of money." (Remember the van, stereos, Porsches?) He also wanted to be with his friends, who were all going to college. In his junior year in high school he decided he would have to pay more attention to grades if he wanted to go to college too. He started studying more, did well on his SATs, was accepted to the University of Massachusetts, majored in business management, and was an A student. Again he was driven to succeed because of a passion—this time it was the desire to get a really great job.

Try This:

Ask your kids what they want to do and then support them in their doing it and being responsible for the outcome. You may want to offer your support by brainstorming with them to come up with various ways they might reach their goals and suggesting people they could contact. The rest is up to them.

Who Do You Know?

We are all interconnected.

They say that if there are six people in a room, you have access to everyone on the planet. Everyone knows someone who knows someone who knows someone—well, you get the idea.

John wanted to be a comedy scriptwriter. When I met with him, he had graduated college and was a production assistant for a radio station. He was working long hours, earning little money, and putting up with abusive management. John had been writing comedy scripts since he was 16. He would often share his ideas with his friends who all thought he was "hysterical." His goal was to write for *Seinfeld* or *Saturday Night Live* but he didn't know how to go about it.

We brainstormed and drew up an action chart like the one on page 177. He needed contacts. I asked him who he knew in the entertainment business or who was a vendor to those businesses (e.g., publishers, advertisers, public relations managers, lawyers, etc.). I also asked him who he knew who might know someone (e.g., neighbors, relatives, barbers, former teachers, etc.). John said he thought that one of his neighbor's sons worked in television in New York. He also talked to his father, an attorney, who knew an entertainment lawyer. We worked on a short introduction he could feel comfortable with: "Hi, my name is John, and I'm a comedy scriptwriter. Is this a convenient time for you? I'm networking to connect with people who do this kind of work. Who do you know who works in TV or broadcasting or who might know someone who does?"

John continued contacting people and soon realized he wanted to be in New York. He quit his job at the radio station, moved to Manhattan, and found a job through a temp agency. The agency placed him in the human resources department of a television network. (Coincidence?) He had a prime view of new jobs opening up. He got an apartment with a couple of buddies, and when he wasn't working or networking he was writing scripts. One of John's contacts had connected him with the owners of a start-up production company who were waiting for their writer from California to arrive. They read some of John's work, liked it, and bought a few of his scripts to try him out. Meanwhile, the company he was temping at offered him a full-time job in their personnel department. He decided not to take the position because it was more of a commitment than he wanted to make. He wanted to continue writing and networking.

As luck would have it (luck = preparedness + opportunity), the California writer decided to back out of the production company. The owners called John and asked if he was still interested. John started work as a full-time comedy scriptwriter

John's Action Chart

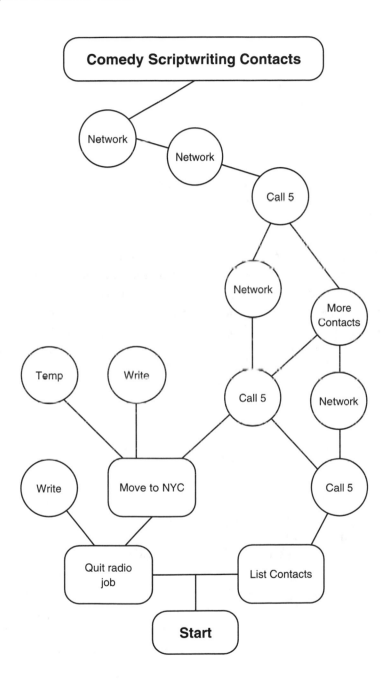

Comedy Scriptwriting Contacts

Network

Network

Call 5

Network

More Contacts

Temp

Write

Call 5

Network

Write

Move to NYC

Call 5

Quit radio job

List Contacts

Start

on salary plus royalties and bonus. This all took place within nine months.

Try This:

To help your kids or friends develop a plan to support their dream, you might start with a map similar to the one John and I created.

Things Take Time

Trust the process.

Too often we worry about whether our kids will be able to support themselves. We sell them short by insisting that they choose the seemingly safe route, which can cost them dearly later. Our children also are frequently tormented by trying to decide what to major in at college to fit into the best career when they graduate. They carry their friends' or our spoken or unspoken expectations to compound their dilemmas.

> Educators and career advisors say a better way is to find a field you're interested in—even passionate about—and major in it. A career will follow. Many students don't understand that one major can often lead to two dozen careers. They'll enroll in business because their uncle suggested it was a good move. Yet they have no idea what majoring in business means. Or they'll express an interest in economics but avoid majoring in it because their parents insist it won't lead to a job.[11]

There are lots of ways to make money. Most of us are unaware of what people do and what they earn. Our scatomas blind us and we don't ask (see Chapter 8). Did you know that a cosmetic salesperson in a department store can make $30,000 a year? A tow-truck driver, the last of the great cowboys, can make $60,000 a year? A film producer makes between $20,000 and $20 million? Teachers make between $25,000 and $60,000? College professors make between $20,000 and $100,000+? Secretaries make between $12,000 and $60,000? Perhaps you'd like to be a musician with a university, an economist who consults to industry, a scientist, an historian with the National Park Service, or a fabric specialist for a chemical company? If you are interested, ask them the salary range.

Today, at 30, Nancy is a successful photographer for a major newspaper. After she graduated college with a major in graphic design, she took a job in a photo lab because she couldn't find work in her field. One day a friend told her that UPI was looking for young photographers. She knocked on the UPI office door and said she was interested. They hired her. Nancy wasn't intimidated that UPI was the largest news agency in the world. She had gone to art school and didn't know what UPI was. Did she make a lot of money in the photo lab? No, but it was the step that led her to an exciting career.

Suzanne went to college for one semester and then dropped out. She had no ambitions. The only thing she liked was music. She would hang out at the clubs listening to the latest groups. Her folks were worried about her. All their other kids were doing well in school and were making plans for their future. Suzanne wasn't. She found a job as a clerk in a music store in the city where she was living. It was a good place to be—"no stress," she said. She could listen to music and be with people her age. It didn't pay much in the beginning, but the management was supportive and kept giving her more responsibility. At the age of 22 she was managing one of their stores. A few years later, the store's business had grown to one of the largest in the state. They had alliances with music companies and were continually offering promotions. When they needed a spotter (a type of talent consultant who would visit clubs and find new talent) they thought of Suzanne. She was a valued part of their company and they trusted her judgment. They offered her the job. Suzanne now hangs out at the clubs, listens to the latest groups, and gets paid well for it. You never know.

Do What *You* Love

In the *Wall Street Journal* (July 31, 1996, B1, p. 1) Sue Shellenbarger reported that in a study of more than 800 managers and professionals, researchers "found fewer behavioral problems in children (4 to 17 years old) whose mothers (and fathers) have control over how, where, and when their work gets done as well as who are satisfied with their work. In the past, most studies about kids and the workplace focused on whether a mother's working outside the home hurts children, a question that is far too simplistic. Jobs differ; some drive you nuts, make you impossible to live with, and pay so little that you can only afford lousy child care. Others lift your self-esteem, impart new skills, and enable you to buy enriching care for your kids."

Share what you've learned from this book. Support your kids, your friends, and your colleagues in being who they are and taking small steps to follow their dreams. Tell them to do work they love where they keep expanding their natural talents and passions and adapt those to the marketplace.

We all have to find our own path. There are no easy answers. What we can do for those we care about is listen to them, love them, be there for them, pray for their best, and do work we love to show them the way.

Aphorisms and Reminders

Start where you are.

You can't *not* use your gifts.

Everything you have done until now has been your training—for the rest of your life.

Tests won't tell you who you are or what you should be. They'll just confirm what you already know.

We are taught that if it's too easy it's unimportant.

Expand and amplify your gifts. Delegate what you don't do easily. This leaves room for you to get better at what you are good at. Naturally.

We live under the spell of our myths—unknowingly.

You can only be what you were designed to be.

What differentiates work from play is you saying so.

The need to have work we love grows as we become older. Not having it can result in paralysis of the spirit.

Do you want to be right or do you want to be happy?

It is always puzzling why we are disappointed when we don't get what we don't want in the first place.

Whenever you find yourself with a negative belief that will keep you from having what you want, say "switch" and state it in the positive. It's your choice.

Your life is your career.

We don't know what we don't know. We have very limited knowledge.

Every job you have should prepare you for the next one somewhere else—even if you choose to stay where you are today.

Working for someone else lulls us into a sense of being taken care of. It is very seductive and dangerous.

Creating safety in the midst of insecurity begins at the personal level. Yours.

Stay away from negative, critical people. Run, don't walk. They only drain your energy.

Do you want to please *everyone* or do you want to be happy?

Helping people help you begins with you being responsible for the outcome. Don't ask for something you need from someone who can't give it to you.

We usually give people permission to not give us what we want. Who are you committed to?

Use words that say, "I'm not kidding," such as *ask, request, propose.*

Set expectations. Let people know what, how, when, and where.

You are 100 percent responsible for ensuring that the other person understands what you are saying.

If you are stressed out, you are not able to do your job, be creative, and support others.

Take a breath break. Notice your body. Stretch. Take a walk.

Look for what's good about . . .

List all the things that bring you joy and include at least one in your life. Daily!

What you need is often what others need too. By honoring yourself, you also honor them.

We are given what we need, not always what we want.

You can reframe your life by refocusing on the positive aspects of all your experiences—including your limitations—how they strengthened you, and what you learned from them.

The only difference between a creative person and a noncreative one is in the saying so.

In this jumbled time of accelerated change, if you can't trust your intuition, what *can* you trust?

Pray, wait, take time to listen to the voice within. And follow that.

Be curious, not smart.

Success depends on being willing to fail—often.

Failure means not reaching the goal you have set for a specific time period. Extend your time period. Or reassess your goal.

Silence your Inner Critic. Be open to new ideas without judgment.

Practice silence, meditate.

To meditate means to be in the present moment.

Surrender to what you're doing when you are doing it.

Imagine that in one year you will have in your life what you desire and your life will have changed. You have been given this time to explore, create, play, and take care of yourself.

You will never be motivated by what you don't want.

The first step in realizing a life dream is in identifying, seeing, and *feeling* it.

Not doing what continually whispers to you to take care of keeps you from having what you really want.

State *how* you want to be, not *what* you want to be.

Choosing doesn't have to be forever.

In order to do something, you first have to become it.

Declare it and make it so.

Act as if the Universe is supporting you.

Don't ask permission. It only gives someone else more work.

Asking permission is giving up your power and not accepting responsibility for the outcome.

Beliefs and appearance are just that.

Your spirit speaks through what calls to you, what you love to do, and where you want to do it.

Your purpose is to share your essence with others.

The answer is showing itself. You just need to receive it.

Listen to your longings.

Love is relevant at work. What is love? Love is patience, respect, honor, care, action, partnership, compassion, helping, welcoming, commitment, and keeping your word.

You will experiment and tumble. Try things on until you find the right fit.

Success does not depend on how you feel.

It's loving what you do that will get you through the hard times.

You are always committing to what you want.

Respect procrastination. It serves and protects you.

When you are clear about your intention and focus your energy and actions on the results you want, miracles happen.

We want it all. Instantly.

Get support. Don't do it alone.

Program your body to revitalize your mind.

In the motivational race between pleasure and pain, pain wins.

Make being uncomfortable more uncomfortable where failure is not an option.

Ask the Universe to give you a sign that you are on the right path.

You *always* have choices.

You are in charge.

If you don't let people know who you are and how you can help them, how will they know?

There is so little we can control in our lives. Sometimes it is limited to what we put on and in our bodies and minds.

People want to help you. Make this your mantra.

Networking is building relationships, asking for advice or help, and *giving back*.

You will encounter resistance. So what?

Expect a screener.

"No" doesn't need to mean forever.

For a "yes," give a choice of two.

The less you say, the more powerful you appear.
It takes at least five contacts for people to trust you.
People hire people they feel safe with.
Allow room for flow.
Provide a service, solve their problems.
Don't highlight what you don't want to do.
Support your kids and friends as they are.
Don't fix what ain't broken.
Things take time.
Love them, yourself, and trust in the process.
Do work you love where you keep expanding your natural
    talents and passions and adapt *those* to the marketplace.
    That's your competitive edge.

Notes

1. Michael Ray and Rochelle Myers, *Creativity in Business* (New York: Doubleday, 1989), p. 114.

2. Arthur F. Miller and Ralph T. Mattson, *The Truth About You: You Were Born for a Purpose* (Old Tappan, NJ: Fleming H. Revell Co., 1977), p. 16.

3. Joe Dominguez and Vicki Robin, *Your Money or Your Life* (New York: Penguin Books, 1993).

4. Ibid.

5. Lynn Brenner, "What People Earn," *Parade Magazine*, 23 June 1996.

6. Joseph Campbell and Bill Moyers, *The Power of Myth* (New York: Doubleday, 1988).

7. Jack Hawley, *Reawakening the Spirit of Work* (New York: Fireside, 1995), p. 99.

8. Mark Canfield and Mark Hansen, *Chicken Soup for the Soul* (Deerfield Beach, FL: Health Communications, 1993), pp. 228–230.

9. Faith Popcorn and Lys Marigold, *Clicking* (New York: HarperCollins, 1996), p. 88.

10. Paul Edwards and Sarah Edwards, *Finding Your Perfect Work* (New York: Tarcher/Putnam, 1996), p. 142.

11. Bob Weinstein, "No Major Yet? Not to Worry. There's Time," *Boston Globe* 6 August 1996, sec. 1.

Recommended Reading

Here are some books I like to recommend to my clients. They are full of practical, inspiring information. They are also creative, well written, and easy to read. I hope you enjoy them.

On Career Development

Boldt, Laurence G. *Zen and the Art of Making a Living. A Practical Guide to Creative Career Design* (New York: Penguin Group, 1993).

Bolles, Richard Nelson. *What Color Is Your Parachute?* (Berkeley, CA: Ten Speed Press, 1996).

Jarow, Rick. *Creating the Work You Love: Courage, Commitment and Career* (Rochester, VT: Destiny Books, 1995).

Sher, Barbara. *I Could Do Anything, If I Only Knew What It Was* (New York: Delacorte Press, 1994).

Sinetar, Marsha. *To Build the Life You Want, Create the Work You Love* (New York: St. Martins Press, 1995).

Yate, Martin. *Knock 'Em Dead: The Ultimate Job-Seeker's Handbook* (Holbrook, MA: Adams Media, 1997).

On Creativity

Cameron, Julia. *The Artist's Way: A Spiritual Path to Higher Creativity* (New York: Jeremy Tarcher/Perigee Books, 1992).

Fritz, Robert. *Creating* (New York: Fawcett Columbine, 1991).

———. *The Path of Least Resistance* (Salem, MA: DMA, 1984).

Kushner, Ray Anthony and Malcolm. *High-Octane Selling: Boost Your Creative Power to Close More Sales* (New York: AMA-COM, 1995).

Leland, Nita. *The Creative Artist: A Fine Artist's Guide to Expanding Your Creativity* (Minneapolis: North Light Books, 1990).

Myers, Michael Ray and Rochelle. *Creativity in Business* (New York: Doubleday, 1989).

Von Oech, Roger. *A Whack on the Side of the Head, a Kick on the Seat of the Pants* (New York: Warner Books, 1990).

———. *Creative Whack Pack* (Stamford, CT: US Games Systems, 1992).

Wujec, Tom. *Pumping Ions: Games and Exercises to Flex Your Mind* (New York: Doubleday, 1988).

Wycoff, Joyce. *Mindmapping: Your Personal Guide to Exploring Creativity and Problem-Solving* (New York: Berkley Books, 1987).

On Future Trends and Creative Work Options

Edwards, Paul and Sarah. *Finding Your Perfect Work* (New York: Tarcher/Putnam, 1996).

Edwards, Paul and Sarah. *Secrets of Successful Self-Employment: Moving from Paycheck Thinking to Profit Thinking* (New York: Simon and Schuster, 1996).

Popcorn, Faith, and Lys Marigold. *Clicking* (New York: Harper-Collins, 1996).

On Intuition

Emery, Marcia. *Intuition Workbook* (Englewood Cliffs, NJ: Prentice Hall, 1994).

Jackson, Gerald. *The Inner Executive: Access Your Intuition for Business Success* (New York: Pocket Books, 1988).

Vaughan, Francis. *Awakening Intuition* (New York: Anchor Books, 1979).

On Marketing Yourself or Your Business

Levinson, Jay Conrad. *Guerrilla Marketing: Secrets for Making Big Profits from Your Small Business* (New York: Houghton Mifflin, 1993).

Michaels, Nancy. *How to Be a Big Fish in Any Pond: Self-Marketing Strategies for Entrepreneurial Success* (audiotape) (Impression Impact, 1994).

Yudkin, Marcia. *6 Steps to Free Publicity and Dozens of Other Ways to Win Free Media Attention for You or Your Business* (New York: Plume-Penguin, 1984).

On Meditating

Kabat-Zinn, Jon. *Wherever You Go, There You Are: Mindfulness Meditation in Everyday Life* (New York: Hyperion, 1994).

Nhat Hanh, Thich. *The Miracle of Mindfulness: A Manual on Meditation* (Boston: Beacon Press, 1987).

On Money

Chopra, Deepak. *The Seven Spiritual Laws of Success* (San Rafael, CA: New World Library, 1994).

Dominguez, Joe, and Vicki Robin. *Your Money or Your Life* (New York: Penguin Books, 1992).

Roman, Sanaya, and Duane Packer. *Creating Money* (Tiburon, CA: HJKramer, 1988).

On Self-Knowledge

Hoff, Benjamin. *The Tao of Pooh* (New York: Penguin Books, 1982).

Kauffman, Barry Neil. *Happiness Is a Choice* (New York: Fawcett Columbine, 1991).

Miller, Arthur, and Ralph Mattson. *The Truth About You: You Were Born for a Purpose* (Old Tappan, NJ: Fleming H. Revell, 1977).

Mitchell, Stephen. *Tao Te Ching: A New English Version with Foreword and Notes* (New York: HarperPerennial, 1991).

On Spirit and Work

DeFoore, Bill, and Joan Renesen, eds. *Rediscovering the Soul of Business* (San Francisco: New Leaders Press, 1995).

Harman, Willis. *Global Mind Change: The Promise of the Last Years of the Twentieth Century* (Indianapolis, IN: Knowledge Systems, 1988).

Hawley, Jack. *Reawakening the Spirit of Work* (San Francisco: Barrett-Koehler Publishing, 1993).

Hillman, James. *The Soul's Code: In Search of Character and Calling* (New York: Random House, 1996).

Moore, Thomas. *Care of the Soul* (New York: HarperCollins, 1992).

Senge, Peter M. *The Fifth Discipline: The Art and Practice of the Learning Organization* (New York: Currency Doubleday, 1994).

On Transitions

Bridges, William. *Transitions: Making Sense of Life's Changes* (Reading, MA: Addison Wesley, 1980).

Handy, Charles. *The Age of Unreason* (Cambridge: Harvard Business School Press, 1989).

Zelinski, Ernie J. *The Joy of Not Working* (Berkeley, CA: Ten Speed Press, 1997).

On Writing Book Proposals

Herman, Jeff, and Deborah Adams. *Write the Perfect Book Proposal* (New York: John Wiley & Sons, 1993).

Larsen, Michael. *How to Write a Book Proposal* (Cincinnati, OH: Writer's Digest Books, 1984).

On Writing for Magazines and Newspapers

Hedette, Jean M., ed. *Handbook of Magazine Article Writing* (Cincinnati, OH: Writer's Digest Books, 1990).

Wood, John. *How to Write Attention-Grabbing Query and Cover Letters* (Cincinnati, OH: Writer's Digest Books, 1996).

Yudkin, Marcia. *Freelance Writing for Magazines and Newspapers* (New York: Harper & Row, 1988).

Every writer I have read, every course I have attended, every wise teacher I have listened to is a part of me. Many of them have been my counselors, my mentors, my coaches, and my spiritual healers. Many have supported and nourished me on my search for work I love. I acknowledge them all with much gratitude and love. I list some of them below:

Melodie Beatty

Warren Bennis

Herbert Benson

Richard Bolles &
 John Christian

Laurence Boldt

Joan Borysenko

Nathaniel Brandon

William Bridges

Juliet Brudney

Martin Buber

David D. Burns

Tony Buzan

Julia Cameron

Joseph Campbell

Jack Canfield

Dale Carnegie

Sri Chimnoy

Pema Chodron

Deepak Chopra

Stephen Covey
The Dalai Lama
Amrit Desai
Joe Dominguez &
  Vicki Robin
Meister Eckhard
Paul & Sarah Edwards
Werner Erhard
Ralph Waldo Emerson
Rita Fischer
Viktor Frankl
Betty Friedan
Robert Fritz
Shakti Gawain
Eugene Gendlin
Natalie Goldberg
John Gray
Dag Hammarksjöld
Charles Handy
Willis Harman
Helen Hawes
Jack Hawley
Margaret Hennig
Abraham Joshua Heschel
James Hillman
Richard Hittleman
Carol Horney
Rick Jarrow
Susan Jeffers
C. G. Jung
Jon Kabat-Zinn
Barry Neil Kaufmann
Sri Khanna
Kripalu Yoga Center
Krishnamurti

Rabbi Harold Kushner
Rabbi Laurence Kushner
Landmark Education
  Foundation
Stephen Levine
Maxwell Maltz
Abraham Maslow
Rollo May
Milton Mayeroff
Pia Melodie
Arthur F. Miller &
  Ralph T. Mattson
Marsha Moore
Thomas Moore
Bill Moyers
Thich Nhat Hanh
James Ogilvy
M. Scott Peck
Fritz Perls
Tom Peters
Faith Popcorn
Ram Das
Michael Ray &
  Rochelle Myers
Sogyal Rinpoche
Anthony Robbins
Sanaya Roman
Virginia Satir
Peter Senge
Barbara Sher
Bernie Siegel
Jose Silva
Marsha Sinetar
Huston Smith
Jess Stearn

Gloria Steinem

Justin Sterling

Shunryu Suzuki

Deborah Tannen

Paul Tillich

Lao Tsu

Frances Vaughan

Roger Von Oech

Alan Watts

Ernie Zelinski

Index

My Bio

Cheryl Gilman has been coaching people on creating new possibilities since she can remember. An advocate of the body-mind connection, she officially started coaching and leading seminars after 20 years in corporate America and a lifetime of yoga and meditation. Her work has been written about in major New England newspapers and has developed a successful following. Clients include Interface in Newton, Massachusetts, The New York Open Center in Manhattan, and major corporations and academic institutions throughout the United States. She also produces and writes a newsletter, *Vitality in Work & Life*, and has written articles on vitality, creativity, careers, and intuition.

She established Cheryl Gilman Associates, a coaching and training company, in 1993 to support people with innovative ways to have what they want in their lives, businesses, and careers.

Her background includes senior management positions for a Fortune 100 company, her own employment consulting firm, and developing sales and marketing programs for start-up organizations. She has delivered outplacement seminars and has recruited and coached all levels of personnel. She speaks French and Spanish and has directed programs in Europe, Canada, Asia, and South America. She has also taught yoga and meditation.

Cheryl has a bachelor of arts degree in languages from the University of Massachusetts and has done postgraduate work in the areas of management, communications, and leadership. She has two grown children and lives in Belmont, Massachusetts.

Cheryl Gilman